I0235657

IMAGES
of America

REDMOND

ON THE COVER: Cars came early to Redmond, considering its unpaved and dusty roads. Among the men in this photograph are driver Jim Toney and J. D. Butler, owner of Redmond Pharmacy, riding shotgun. An August 1, 1912, issue of the *Spokesman* touted two car tourists from Washington state passing through town "enroute to Bend in a 58 horse power Stoddard Dayton car. They are pleased with this section and think Redmond has a great future." (Redmond Historical Commission.)

IMAGES
of America

REDMOND

Leslie Pugmire Hole and Trish Pinkerton

ARCADIA
PUBLISHING

Copyright © 2009 by Leslie Pugmire Hole and Trish Pinkerton
ISBN 978-1-5316-4647-9

Published by Arcadia Publishing
Charleston, South Carolina

Library of Congress Control Number: 2009924712

For all general information contact Arcadia Publishing at:
Telephone 843-853-2070
Fax 843-853-0044
E-mail sales@arcadiapublishing.com
For customer service and orders:
Toll-Free 1-888-313-2665

Visit us on the Internet at www.arcadiapublishing.com

To my late mother, Grace Lee Hudson Miller, who was born
in Redmond in 1926 and even after moving away never lost her
love for juniper, sage, and mountains on the horizon –TLP

To the people of Redmond—past, present, and future—as
well as my family, who tolerated with good humor my frequent
absences and obsession with Redmond's history –LPH

CONTENTS

ACKNOWLEDGMENTS

A funny thing happened on the way to compiling photographs for this book. As we searched our archives, very much like a small town in its casual organization, we discovered that many of our newspaper photographs were also in personal family collections and the files of local historical organizations, among other places. And some photographs in our files appeared to have originated from outside the newspaper.

So we preface this book with preemptive apologies for any incorrect attribution of the origin of any photographs used; even though we worked hard to determine ownership of images, mistakes are likely.

We also feel compelled to express regrets for any omissions in the topics contained in this book; it is remarkable that 100 short years of history could contain so much more information than we could include. At times, we had great historical information but no photograph to illustrate it, despite our best efforts to find one.

This book was a collaborative process, with limitless teamwork between its authors and the city of Redmond. Special thanks need to be given to our publisher, Gary Husman, who blessed the project with his support and periodic dispensation from our daily jobs.

The authors would have had a much more difficult task had it not been for two previous books on Redmond's history, *Redmond, Rose of the Desert* by B. Elizabeth Ward and *Redmond, Where the Desert Blooms* by Keith Clark. Both books are now out of print but provided invaluable background into our community's history.

The bulk of our research, however, came from the archives of our newspaper, the *Redmond Spokesman*. While most of its 100 years of publication are available on microfiche, we preferred to peruse the pages of the dusty bound volumes, searching for clues to unravel the story of our town.

Many of our readers contributed to this book as well, by sharing photographs, stories, or historical background. We reached out to them early in the process of compiling this book, and they opened their lives and family histories to us. A special thanks needs to be given for their generosity.

INTRODUCTION

Prior to the beginning of the 20th century, Central Oregon was viewed by most as a place to keep a visit short. The high desert seemed inhospitable to all except the native peoples, who knew where to find shelter and food. With the exception of the burgeoning town of Prineville, nestled in a sheltered valley along the Crooked River, little settlement was taking place in the region during the era when the rest of the West was filling up.

Central Oregon was a blank spot on the map of Oregon, even 40 years after statehood. The 1894 Carey Act, allowing private development of irrigation systems through arid federal land—and more importantly, allowing states to dole out that land to homesteaders—changed everything.

Within the first few years of the new century, wagons began rolling into Central Oregon, and the spot that was to become Redmond, still dry as a bone and at more than 3,000 feet of elevation, was smack in the middle of it all.

At one time Prineville, the first incorporated town in the region, was the epicenter of the region due to its designation as the county seat. But when the Oregon Trunk Railroad chose in 1911 to bring its line from The Dalles through to Redmond instead of Prineville, the "Hub of Central Oregon" was crowned.

The first settlers, the hardy souls who set up housekeeping before the canals brought water in 1906, lived in tents and hauled water from the Deschutes River 4 miles away. All supplies had to be hauled by horse and mule teams from Shaniko, 75 miles north, where the rail line ended at that time. Everyone knew the water was coming, and hopefully the railroad right behind, and speculation on what land would be valuable sustained them through some rough years.

While the city's early years saw the building of numerous churches (only the historic Presbyterian church is still standing), those first decades also brought saloons, moonshiners, houses of ill repute, and gambling, due in large part to the influx of workers for canal and railroad construction.

Once founded on farming and ranching and later bolstered by lumber mills, the city of Redmond and surrounding areas today also boast light industrial, manufacturing, and technology-based businesses, as well as a highly respected fair and expo center and busy regional airport. The local school district and a top-rated hospital are among the area's largest employers.

Redmond has been known through the years for its railroad, potato industry, and passion for rodeo and all things Western, but mostly for its serendipitous location: squarely in the center of the region and equidistant from the other four major towns that make up Central Oregon.

For many decades, Redmond progressed at a steady pace, punctuated with small booms and busts, similar to other towns in the West. The Cascades cut the city off from the more populous Willamette Valley, and residents were content making a living at farming, ranching, or any of the other shorter-lived industries such as mining, turkey farming, and mill work.

The Redmond-area population was boosted by smaller endeavors, such as the Civilian Conservation Corps camp begun in 1939, a World War II–era military airbase, and through the years by outlying unincorporated communities such as Terrebonne, Lower Bridge, Crooked River Ranch, Eagle Crest, and Powell Butte.

Beginning in the late 1980s, Central Oregon began to be discovered by people looking for a great climate and wonderful outdoor recreation choices. The population in Redmond and surrounding areas doubled and then doubled again in a few short decades. Neighborhoods sprang up where farms once stood, and the number of cars coming through town brought traffic nearly to a standstill on busier days.

On a more whimsical note, Redmond is infamous in the annals of UFO history as the site of one of the best-documented sightings in the 20th century, a 1959 event that scrambled U.S. Air Force jets and is still talked about by those curious about extraterrestrial life.

For many years, even after the industry declined, Redmond held a Potato Festival that attracted thousands to town and celebrated all things tuber. In its earliest incarnation, the festival was connected with the county fair, but in 1958, the year before Redmond helped Oregon celebrate its centennial by creating a false-fronted downtown renamed Juniper Junction, the Potato Festival was set apart and given its own honored week in late September, after harvest.

Redmond was also the site of one of the West's ever-popular golden spike ceremonies, commemorating the arrival of the winning rail line after a contentious race to town from rival railroad barons Hill and Harriman.

There has never been a shortage of interesting people in Redmond, interesting both for their impact on the town and simply for who they were. Businessman J. R. Roberts helped mold a regional airport from what was a World War II–era airbase; eccentric farmer Rasmus Petersen put Redmond on the map with his 4-acre rock garden built in his spare time; Samuel Johnson and his wife, Becky, dominated the political and civic climate in the city for many decades; and former Lower Bridge resident and World War II flyer Rex T. Barber is credited with shooting down Admiral Yamamoto, architect of the Peal Harbor attack. Former Oregon governor Tom McCall graduated from Redmond Union High School and grew up on a farm outside of town. Longtime *Spokesman* publisher Mary Brown was a complicated lady with a simple name, as she was hard drinking, straight talking, and fiercely loyal to Redmond and the journalism industry. She ran the paper for many decades in an era when few women had a career, especially those in a small town.

In and around Redmond are Smith Rock State Park, a world-renowned climbing destination and recreation spot that receives upwards of several million visitors a year; Cline Falls, a narrow gorge watercourse that was dammed for electrical power in the early 1900s and supported a community of its own for a short time; the 1911 railroad bridge; the 1926 Crooked River High Bridge and its replacement, the Rex T. Barber Bridge, which sit side by side across the narrow 300-foot-deep Crooked River Canyon; Dry Canyon, a prehistoric riverbed that bisects Redmond north to south and now hosts parks and trails (and was once the site of the town garbage dump); Redmond Caves, actually a series of collapsed lava tubes, which have been excavated numerous times for Native American artifacts and lie within city limits; Operation Santa Claus, the only operating reindeer ranch in the lower 48; and of course the aforementioned Petersen Rock Garden, a must-see on any roadside attraction list.

If Redmond could be said to be known for any one thing, that might be dogged persistence. A lack of water or transportation did not dissuade its earlier settlers and townsfolk through the years; they resolutely bounced back from collapsed industries like mining, turkey farming, potato farming, and the wood products industry.

The town that has sometimes been portrayed as the mousey little sister to its more glamorous neighbor, Bend, has steadfastly refused to be stereotyped and continues to seek ways to both reinvent itself and remain true to its roots.

One

THE HUB OF CENTRAL OREGON

Dirt streets required much maintenance for the new city, as evidenced in this 1911 photograph of Sixth Street. An item in the April 4, 1912, *Spokesman* noted, "The street sprinkler was out last Thursday afternoon. The wind blew the dust in clouds and Marshal McClay gained the goodwill of the merchants by getting the water cart out and wetting down the principal business streets." (Tonia Kissler Cain.)

Before the railroad came to Central Oregon, Glen Ridgeway (pictured) of Lamonta hauled freight between the railhead at Shaniko and Central Oregon. The trip was often slow, on narrow dirt tracks and through dust and mud. It sometimes took wagons eight hours just to get through Cow Canyon north of Madras. In 2007, Ridgeway descendants told their family story to the *Spokesman*. When pioneer settlers Frank and Josephine Redmond needed lumber for their first home, they

flagged down Glen Ridgeway. One day in 1904, as Glen was on one of his runs, a man who needed lumber to build a house stopped him. That man was Frank Redmond, and Ridgeway ended up bringing him the lumber. "Without a house Frank Redmond might not have stayed," said Joanne Luke of Bend, one of Ridgeway's granddaughters. (Ridgeway family.)

Joe McClay (below, in about 1910) arrived in Central Oregon with his family around 1905, where he worked with his father, Z. T., building irrigation canals, running the livery stable behind the Hotel Redmond, and hauling freight. Father and son are pictured on the wooden sidewalks of Redmond (above) around the same time; Joe is second from left and Z. T. is fourth from left. In a 1974 interview, Joe recalled that one time, as his stage was descending Trail Crossing, the brakes gave out. He finally got the horse stopped with the stage and passengers in one piece, but "I was cussed all the way down for being a Wild West driver. One old guy jumped out and gave me the devil. I told him he wasn't a bit scareder than I was, and you and I ought to be thankful we got down the hill straight up." (Both McClay family.)

Z. T. and Mary McClay, pictured here, had a home on Eighth Street with bountiful gardens during the second decade of the 20th century. An item in the July 8, 1915, *Spokesman* noted, "Mrs. Z. T. McClay sent a nice sweet smelling bouquet of sweet peas and pinks that she grew in her garden to the Spokesman office Tuesday morning for which she has our thanks." (McClay family.)

E Street, now Evergreen Avenue, stretches east from Sixth Street in this 1911 photograph. The far building on the left housed Tum-A-Lum Lumber. The large building to its left was a livery stable that was destroyed in a spectacular fire in 1912. As the *Redmond Spokesman* reported in its July 4 issue, that fire destroyed "J. H. Vincent's large livery and feed barn, 10 head of horses, a stallion valued at $4,000, two wagon-loads of furniture and a $5,000 box of silverware, paintings and wedding presents belonging to E. A. McCall, son-in-law of Thomas Lawson, who is building a mansion on his ranch on Crooked River near this city. . . . Owing to absence of wind and by good work on the part of the firemen the large plant of the Tum-A-Lum Lumber Co., across the street from the livery barn was saved." (Redmond Historical Commission.)

During the summer of 1913, Nell Irwin holds daughter Ruth outside the family's new home in Redmond (above). The elms planted around the yard (visible in foreground) were among the many Irwin planted or encouraged to be planted in Redmond over the next several decades. The August 10, 1911, *Spokesman* stated, "CH Irwin has the lumber on the ground for a six-room bungalow he will build on his block of lots in Ellinger's Addition. The building is to have the latest modern improvements." Within a few years, the family painted the home and added a porch (below). Visible in front is the dirt road that would become Northwest Seventh Street. (Both Ruth Ann Hartley.)

Irrigation water was the key to farming the high desert. In 1908, the Sears clan gathered for a picnic at the new flume that delivered water to Powell Butte. Pictured from left to right are D. A. Yates, Guy Sears, Mrs. Yates, Alice Sears, Mrs. Guy Sears with baby Doris, Sarah Wilcox, M. K. Uland, Verne Sears, Orissa Sears, Ada Sears, and Kilman Uland. (Redmond Historical Commission.)

Tent houses were popular residences in Redmond's early days when lumber was scarce. Pictured in 1911 is Lora Smith with her nieces and nephew, from left to right, Evelyn, Helen, and Philo Smith. A classified advertisement in the July 27, 1911, *Spokesman* read, "FOR SALE–The best built, most complete tent house in town; also household goods, corner Third and E streets. Inquire of Miss Jones or Jones Land Co." (Redmond Historical Commission.)

George and Bertha Elliott and son Lester pose in 1910 on the north side of Tetherow (Cinder) Butte. Bertha was the first schoolteacher in Terrebonne, and George was a farmer and freight wagon driver. The May 10, 1934, *Spokesman* mentioned their fourth child, Maxine, as she edged out Clyde Martin for salutatorian honors for the Redmond Union High School class of 1934. Two years earlier, Clyde's sister Evelyn had beaten Sid, Maxine's brother. (Elliott family.)

Hotel Redmond at the corner of E Street and Sixth Street was renovated in 1911 for new ownership. A September 7, 1911, *Spokesman* went on to state, "The entire upper floor is devoted to hotel purposes, there being 45 bedrooms, all newly furnished. A Royal Wilton rug covers the floor, comfortable easy chairs are there and a Steinway grand piano occupies a prominent position . . . H. F. Jones is the genial boniface and W. W. Alldrege assists in looking after the patrons of the house and ministering to their wants." (Redmond Historical Commission.)

Before the arrival of the railroad in the fall of 1911, horses and wagons brought heavy loads into Central Oregon. The wagon train pictured here was traveling south to Silver Lake in 1908 to deliver a boiler to a sawmill. The Hotel Redmond livery barn, one of several in town, was in the block west of the hotel. (Redmond Historical Commission.)

The Redmond Grill on Sixth Street served diners on the first floor and rented rooms on the second. In early 1912, when this photograph was taken, W. E. Young was the proprietor. In March 7, 1912, the *Spokesman* noted that improvements included plate-glass windows in the front and a doubling of the size of the dining room by tearing out a wall into space previously occupied by Pioneer Meat Market. (Redmond Historical Commission.)

The year 1911 was big for construction in Redmond; pictured is Sixth Street looking north from E Street (Evergreen Avenue.) As the August 10, 1911, *Spokesman* noted, "A walk around the city will soon convince the most skeptical that there is more building going on in Redmond and improvements being made than in any other locality in Central Oregon. This is not mere newspaper talk, but is a fact, borne out by tangible evidence. Every carpenter, mechanic and laborer in the city who wants work can get it, and a good sized payroll is disbursed weekly. Anyone who wants to see a city where things are doing should come to Redmond." (Redmond Historical Commission.)

Redmond's founding shortly after the beginning of the 20th century came at a time when horses were widely used for transportation, freight hauling, and farm work. Kendall and Chapman advertised in the July 13, 1911, *Spokesman* offering a "good line of Studebaker and Bain wagons that we are selling reasonable." Above, freight wagons and townspeople gather outside the Hotel Redmond in 1908 with driver Bill Buckley. Frank McCaffery, real estate agent, farmer, and businessman, is in the center of the three men standing. At the same time more automobiles were arriving. The August 24, 1911, *Spokesman* noted, "E. L. Rapp, H. J. Love and F. I. Phoenix returned Saturday night from an auto trip to Paisley, about 180 miles south of here." Below, stage owners Jess Tetherow (left of truck, hand on fender) and John Hunsaker (right of truck, hand on frame) prepare to begin a route between Redmond and Prineville in 1912. (Both Redmond Historical Commission.)

Work on the foundation for Redmond's stone passenger depot began in November 1911. By December, stonecutters were at work seven days a week. In addition, crews built a cottage for the station agent, two section houses, a freight warehouse, and a big water tank. In March 1912, the railroad announced special fares to all Central Oregon points: from Chicago, $33; St. Paul, $25; Des Moines, $27.85; New York, $50; Milwaukee, $31.50. (Redmond Historical Commission.)

Snow blankets Sixth Street in downtown Redmond during the big snow of 1919. The December 11, 1919, *Spokesman* reported that "with real Redmond enterprise, the city marshal yesterday began the work of clearing trails throughout the city, using six and eight horses, so that anyone reaching the town from the outside will be able to negotiate on streets with horse or team." (Ruth Ann Hartley).

Two

BUILDING A COMMUNITY

From late 1911 until the mid-1960s, passenger trains connected Redmond residents with the world. On October 3, 1963, the *Spokesman* reported that "third grade pupils from [Bend schools] took the annual passenger train excursion from Bend to Redmond . . . total number of youngsters taking the trip was 374. The purpose is in connection with a transportation program being held at the schools." (Redmond Historical Commission.)

The early 20th century Trail Crossing road and river-level bridge was replaced in 1925 by an all-steel span locals would call High Bridge. A *Spokesman* story just prior to its July 1925 opening stated, "The completion of this great bridge will mark the culmination of a dream of the Central Oregon people for a number of years and Trail Crossing, that feared of all crossings, will be a thing of the past." (Both Redmond Historical Commission.)

Construction of the railroad bridge over the Crooked River Gorge in 1911 was dangerous work. In the August 31, 1911, *Spokesman* it was reported, "In some manner the steel slipped and nearly knocked Mr. Adams from his position. . . . By a lucky chance the foreman caught himself and escaped unhurt, though somewhat shocked. Had he fell to the bottom of the canyon he would undoubtedly have been instantly killed on the rocks." (*Spokesman*.)

Construction of the Rex Barber Veterans Memorial Bridge (under construction in rear, after two spans in foreground) was reported in the March 3, 1999, *Spokesman*, "On a blustery afternoon last week Kurt Sayenga and his crew finished filming a segment for a Discovery Channel special scheduled to air in the fall. . . . The film crew shot footage from the edges of the arches that will span the 300-foot-deep gorge." (*Spokesman*.)

The Oregon Trunk Railroad Bridge was finished in 1911 after a competition between railroad barons to bring tracks from The Dalles south into Central Oregon. A 1911 headline in the *Spokesman* read, "Oregon Trunk RR Bridge draws sightseers last week." The front-page story listed more than a dozen Redmond-area families that turned up the day the center arch was installed on the railway bridge. Picnics were laid out along the canyon, and everyone enjoyed themselves immensely. The site continued to be a popular location for recreation and was later the location of the Peter Ogden Skene Scenic Wayside Park. In the photograph, Anna Kissler and Steve Stevens enjoy the view from the top of the canyon sometime in the early 1920s. (Tonia Kissler Cain.)

In April 1912, crews completed construction of Redmond's passenger depot. The community put up the extra $450 to have the building constructed of stone rather than wood. When the depot opened, the *Spokesman* reported that the building was "without question finest on the line." The black-and-white crushed Italian marble terrazzo was deemed a nice effect and indestructible. Outside, all telegraph, telephone, and semaphore lines were installed underground. (Tonia Kissler Cain.)

Burlington Northern stopped using the depot in the mid-1980s. After sitting vacant for years and with pending loss of access due to construction of the Highway 97 reroute, the city purchased the depot from BNSF for $1, and in 2004 crews dismantled it block-by-block and reconstructed it along the railroad tracks at Airport Way. (*Spokesman.*)

No.9. CLINE FALLS AND POWER PLANT, REDMOND, OR.

Cline Falls, Cline Buttes, and a now-extinct community were named for pioneer dentist Dr. Cass A. Cline. In the early years of the 20th century, the town of Cline Falls on the west side of the Deschutes River boasted a post office, two stores, a meat market, livery stable, two hotels, a land sales office, a newspaper, school, a power plant, and 500 platted lots. The town began its decline once the railroad chose a route on the east side of the river through to Redmond in 1911. (Tonia Kissler Cain.)

A combination of ditches and flumes brought water to Redmond and surrounding areas such as Powell Butte. A quote from September 20, 1917, *Spokesman* stated, "A citizens meeting was held at the community hall Sunday immediately after Sabbath School to discuss the building of the Highline ditch, the North Canal and the stave flume. If this can be done about 12,500 acres not now irrigated can be put under water." (Redmond Historical Commission.)

Most of the region's main canals were installed by mid-century and remained a lifeline for farmers and ranchers. By the 1990s, as subdivisions bloomed like weeds and houses replaced farmers' fields, canals were often in the way. This section of canal along Highway 97 in Redmond ran adjacent to Ray Johnson Park. It was piped and buried in 2004, when a highway reroute required a new configuration of the streets. (*Spokesman*.)

In the 1920s, work crews organized by the American Legion post and the Redmond Commercial Club cleared the land for the original runways at what would become Redmond Municipal Airport. A May 6, 1920, *Spokesman* headline reported, "Redmond people see first airplane in history of city." It continued to inform that C. P. Thompson of the Thompson Aircraft Company arrived with his 110-horsepower Thompson Canuck biplane to give exhibition and passenger flights. (Tonia Kissler Cain.)

During World War II, Redmond's airport was taken over by the U.S. Army Air Corps as a training site. On July 22, 1943, the *Spokesman* reported, "Redmond Army Air Base saw its first fatality resulting from a plane crash Sunday when a four-motored bomber cracked up on the field about 3:30 p.m., Lt. Marion M. Kilian announced." This photograph was taken in 1946, after the U.S. Army abandoned the site. (Redmond Historical Commission.)

Daily air service came to Redmond in 1946, causing quite a surge of pride for local townsfolk. The October 3, 1946, *Spokesman* stated, "To witness United Airlines inauguration of daily air services to the Bend-Redmond stop several thousand Central Oregon residents congregated Tuesday morning at Roberts Field. . . . Each passenger and crew on the first plane received a gift box of Deschutes Netted Gem potatoes." Pictured in the foreground from left to right are Redmond Airport Commission members J. F. Short, Ralph Hauck, and J. R. Roberts and United Station manager James Fogarty. (*Spokesman*.)

From left to right, Queen Barbara Stickland and her court, Princess Vicki McNulty and Rita Young, light the Progress Torch at the entrance to the Deschutes County Fairgrounds for the 1969 golden anniversary of the fair. The 22-foot-tall torch was built by Cascade Natural Gas Company in 1964 and was topped with an old wagon wheel. It was torn down when the fairgrounds were relocated in 1999. (*Spokesman.*)

In 1921, Redmond was officially designated by the state as the site of the county fair. In that year, the poultry building was erected along with stock pens and a bucking chute. The fairgrounds grew to include a racetrack and many more buildings. On May 6, 1920, the *Spokesman* reported that a new 1,200-seat grandstand was nearing completion and that "more than 40 businessmen donned overalls Tuesday afternoon and grubbed sagebrush off the fairgrounds, which are being improved this spring." By the late 1980s, when the photograph above was taken, the popular summer event had begun to outgrow the site, and plans began to relocate the fairgrounds. Seen below, the new Deschutes County Fairgrounds and Expo Center, south of the airport, opened in 1999. The 132-acre modern facility replaced the longtime fairgrounds, which were sited where the Fred Meyer shopping center is currently located. (Both *Spokesman.*)

Nurses from Central Oregon District Hospital (CODH), built in 1952, pose for a photograph in the mid-1950s. Helen Scheel (first row, second from left) was the new hospital's only surgical nurse. If a surgical emergency occurred when she was off her shift, and the hospital could not reach her by phone, the on-duty policeman would be dispatched to find her. The small hospital's few doctors acted as surrogate fathers during school functions for Donna and sister Carol, as their parents were divorced. (Donna Scheel Boehm.)

Central Oregon District Hospital underwent another expansion in the 1980s, pictured here. The original building opened in August 1952 after about four years of work by supporters to create the hospital district, including getting the state legislature to pass a law allowing the formation of hospital districts. In 2002, CODH merged with St. Charles Medical Center in Bend and took the St. Charles name. (*Spokesman.*)

Nurse Helen Scheel (first row, far right) smiles in this undated photograph with Central District Hospital staff. A story from the September 15, 1960, *Spokesman* regarding new practical nurses' training held by Central Oregon College, in which five students from Redmond were enrolled, stated, "Following the four-week clinical training period, the students are then assigned to one of the three hospitals where they take their supervised on-the-job training." (Donna Scheel Boehm.)

Redmond was home to a Civilian Conservation Corps camp, built on land just northwest of the airport. In the October 20, 1938, *Spokesman* a story stated, "Mayor E. C. Parker today proclaimed an official holiday for Redmond between the hours of 2 and 4 during the CCC camp (grand opening) ceremonies and urged that everyone who can possibly do so close up shop and take part in the event." Camp Redmond was designed to house 600 men, with 12 barracks, a heating plant, supply depot, commissary, and laundry. Enrollees were paid $30 a month ($22 of that going to their families, if on relief). In 1939, one company from Camp Redmond began work on a new stretch of the North Unit irrigation canal. The onset of World War II ended the work, which would not be completed until 1946. By 1942, Camp Redmond was empty. (Both Redmond Historical Commission.)

In July 1965, the *Spokesman* ran this photograph of a smoke jumper training at Redmond Air Center, which the Forest Service had opened the year before on the north side of the airport. On July 29, 1965, the *Spokesman* reported, "Redmond Air Center dispatched 52 smokejumpers to 25 lightning-caused fires from Saturday evening to Tuesday morning. . . . To date the center has dropped men at 42 fires this year. A total of 268 jumps have been made, including training jumps, and there have been no injuries." (*Spokesman*.)

Laura T. Jones, sister of the second mayor of Redmond, Howard Jones, began a small lending library with her own books in early Redmond. Ladies took turns as librarian, and the collection moved all over town before landing in a room at city hall in 1937. By 1972, the library moved to a 2,000-square-foot building that it was to outgrow within 20 years. After two failed bond measures, the city was able to fund a renovation of the former Jessie Hill Elementary School in 1995 and move into an 18,000-square-foot facility. The school closure was made possible by the construction of the new Vern Patrick Elementary in southwest Redmond. (Both *Spokesman*.)

In 1941, the city of Redmond built an outdoor swimming pool in Ray Johnson Park, which lay next to the Pilot Butte Canal (corner left in the above photograph). The project was headed by the Kiwanis Club and funded mostly through private donations. The pool replaced a Depression-era swimming tank with wood walls and a sand floor that was fed by the nearby canal. The pool served the community until an indoor facility was constructed in 1979. A June 3, 1948, *Spokesman* story read, "Undoubtedly the most popular place in town these days is Redmond's municipal pool, which drew a total of 154 swimmers on Tuesday, the opening day. It was the biggest opening the tank ever had." (Both *Spokesman*.)

These images are looking north on Sixth Street around 1943, when it was still a two-way street (above), and in the 1960s after it was switched to a one-way road (below). Redmond finally gave up living with the growing traffic coming through town on Highway 97—Sixth Street while it was downtown—in 1951. The city opted to turn Fifth and Sixth Streets into a couplet, with northbound highway traffic on Fifth Street and southbound on Sixth Street. On-street parking remained on both roads. An article states from the June 21, 1951, *Spokesman*, "Residents have accepted the new driving pattern with almost a holiday spirit. Shouts of glee go up when an occasional car gets trapped in the wrong direction, although surprisingly few are going astray, according to Sixth Street observers." By 2008, the city was fed up with high traffic counts again, and a highway bypass route was opened east of downtown. (Both *Spokesman*.)

Three

NOTABLE PEOPLE

Frank and Josephine Redmond came to Oregon in 1901 from North Dakota with their daughter Lucile. For the first three years they lived in Wasco, where Frank was a school principal (Josephine was also a teacher). In 1904, the couple moved south to homestead a dry-land section next to what they hoped would be a new irrigation canal and rail line. For two years, they hauled water from the Deschutes River several miles away, eventually building a farmhouse and outbuildings that would be bordered on each side by the canal and railroad. In later years, the Redmonds owned and operated Oregon Hotel, which was destroyed in 1927. A September 21, 1933, *Spokesman* article states, "Mr. and Mrs. Redmond exhibited the greatest number of farm products in the first (1906) and second fairs. Redmond says his keenest competition was from the experimental farm cultivated by the irrigation company financing the fair project." (Redmond Historical Commission.)

Frank McCaffery, originally from New York, came to what would become Redmond in 1905 with his wife, Minnie, and son Fred. McCaffery, a farmer, developer, and real estate agent of great renown, probably bought and sold much of Redmond by the time of his death in 1955. This photograph of McCaffery, taken around 1910 and used in a promotional brochure, aimed to lure buyers to Redmond for real estate. (*Spokesman.*)

Maurice A. "Mike" Lynch came to Redmond in 1910 and partnered with J. R. Roberts in the Lynch and Roberts store that was a fixture of downtown Redmond for several decades. Like Roberts, Lynch was active in civic affairs. He pushed for better roads, state parks, and economic development, served on the state wildlife commission, and in the 1930s was a state representative from the Redmond area. (Redmond Historical Commission.)

Pioneer merchant J. R. Roberts brought his bride, Oda, to town from Iowa on the first passenger train into Redmond in November 1911. J. R.'s tireless work over the decades, pursuing his vision for the future of aviation in Redmond, put his name on Redmond's airport. Both Oda and J. R. were involved in many civic activities. (Elizabeth Cockerham.)

Family Album

October 25, 1911

We Overlooked

Having This Picture

Taken.

So We Are Having It Made Now

In 1949 to Wish You a

Very Merry Christmas

Oda and Roy

Members of Chad Irvin's male singing quartet gather on Deschutes Avenue in the early 1920s. From left to right are Floyd Barton, Dr. Malick, Chad Irvin, and "Jonesie the Jeweler." As the *Spokesman* reported on July 21, 1938, "Hair on the head of relief officials in Deschutes County, declares Relief Committeeman Chad Irvin, lifts in unison whenever the conversation at a relief meeting swings to the employment outlook here for this winter." (Ruth Ann Hartley.)

Norm Weigand, his brothers Pearl, Jack, and Rolla, and sister Neva (McCaffery) were prominent members of the Redmond area farming and business communities. In September 1938, the *Spokesman* reported, "Each year sees additional potato storage cellars built in the Powell Butte area. Among those under construction at this time is a 56 by 130 foot structure being built jointly by Norman and Rolla Weigand on what is known as the Scheurer place." (Phil Weigand.)

In 1970, then governor of Oregon, Tom McCall (second from right) came home to Redmond to see his mother, Dorothy, for her 80th birthday. They were joined by McCall's siblings. Pictured from left to right are Samuel McCall, Jean Babson, Henry McCall, Dorothy McCall, and Dorothy Chamberlain. McCall shared his childhood between Central Oregon and Massachusetts, where one grandfather was governor and the other a wealthy industrialist. The elder McCalls were known for their progressive ranching techniques, and later Dorothy published a series of memoirs. Tom McCall, a Redmond High School graduate, served as governor from 1967 to 1975. (*Spokesman.*)

Civil War veteran Z. T. McClay, seen at left, and his family arrived in Central Oregon in 1905. He and his son Joe built canals and ran the Redmond Livery Stable during its first year. From 1911 to 1912, Z. T. served as Redmond's town marshal but resigned in 1912, along with the mayor, amid allegations that gambling, drinking, and prostitution were running rampant in Redmond. But he took care of more mundane problems too, as the *Spokesman* noted on August 3, 1911, "Acting City Marshal McClay states that he has given notice to owners of cows in the city that the ordinance relating to cattle running at large will hereafter be strictly enforced." His son Joe was a lifelong resident of the Redmond area. Below, Joe McClay and his grandson Joe play at the family farm just south of Terrebonne around 1940. (Both McClay family.)

John Zumstein was a Swiss immigrant who grew up on a farm in the Willamette Valley. It took trial and error with importing animals from Alaska and Lapland, feeding formulas, caring for their health, and deciding when to transplant for Zumstein to build a reindeer herd in Central Oregon. He became a bit of an expert on transplanting reindeer and traveled to places such as New Zealand and Korea to offer advice on the topic. (*Spokesman.*)

Danish immigrant Rasmus Petersen built a fantasyland of rock work on his farm south of Redmond, turning it into a quirky tourist attraction. But Petersen was also a good farmer. A September 30, 1915, article in the *Spokesman* listed the attributes of a dozen or so local farms and ranches, "Rasmus Petersen ranch: Fine corn and oats and 200-ton crops of alfalfa from 85 acres; very pretty home, well-kept lawn, shade trees, graded walks and hop vines on porch." (*Spokesman.*)

M. W. Pettigrew started his newspaper career in Kansas in 1884 and was editor and publisher of the *Redmond Spokesman* from February 1916 to February 1920. He came to Central Oregon intending to retire to farming but ended up buying the newspaper. After selling the paper, he returned to his interest in agriculture. As the *Spokesman* noted on March 4, 1920, "High class dairy cows in Central Oregon have been increased by the addition of 26 high grade Tillamook stock brought to Redmond last Friday morning by M. W. Pettigrew, former publisher of the *Redmond Spokesman* . . . 'I have realized for a long time,' said Pettigrew, 'that farmers here did not own the class of stuff nor the numbers of dairy animals they wished. I know there is a demand for good stock here and I shipped a car in on the strength of my belief.' " (*Spokesman.*)

Mary Conn Brown and then-husband, Joe C. Brown, purchased the *Redmond Spokesman* in November 1931. Mary secured sole ownership of the paper in 1955 and ran the business until 1971, when she sold it to Western Communications. Mary Brown was known as a character; she was a pilot and mountain climber. As the *Spokesman* printed on July 29, 1937 noted, "Mr. and Mrs. Chal Nooe of Bend and Mrs. Joe C. Brown spent the weekend at Rainier National Park. Mrs. Nooe and Mrs. Brown made the Mt. Rainier summit climb Saturday and Sunday over the new climb route up Cadaver Gap." Brown is pictured here in 1959 with the new press for the paper. (*Spokesman*.)

Former Redmond mayor, Oregon state representative, and philanthropist Samuel S. Johnson was the son of well-to-do California timber baron Col. S. Orie Johnson. He served in the U.S. Army Corps of Engineers during World War II, returned to Redmond to run several lumber and sawmill operations in the region, and later served in the Oregon Legislature. When Johnson died in 1984 during his third term as Redmond's mayor, the *Spokesman* dedicated nearly two full pages of news to his passing. His list of professional and community service positions alone took up a quarter of a page. A June 27, 1984, editorial stated in part, "Johnson was quick with a smile, a joke or a brusque command. . . . In his obituary 'Mr.' is out of place and totally inadequate. He was 'Sam' to everybody." In the undated photograph below, Johnson is visiting with the unidentified Redmond Potato Festival king and queen. (Both *Spokesman*.)

The wife of Sam Johnson, the former Redmond mayor, Elizabeth H. "Becky" Johnson became the queen of civic service in the community. A Midwest native who moved to Redmond with her husband after World War II, Johnson raised two daughters while managing to serve on enough boards, committees, commissions, and task forces that it took more than five pages to list them when she died in 2007. Johnson, a teacher prior to her service in the U.S. Navy, did not limit her interests. She gave service to health care, forestry, politics, economic development, senior issues, charitable foundations, history, and education. Her dedication, passion, and razor-sharp memory were well known in the community. (*Spokesman.*)

Hugh Hartman joined the Redmond Grade School District in 1947, and for the next 23 years he was a force in Redmond education and the community. In 1965, Hartman became superintendent of both the grade and union high school districts. He supervised the building of John Tuck, Brown, and Lynch Elementary Schools and Redmond High School. He was active in civic affairs, including the Potato Festival, the Buckaroo Breakfast, and Kiwanis. (Vernon Giles.)

Anna Kissler came to Redmond in 1913 after her first husband died in Iowa, and she married Walter Curtiss on April 30, 1921, her parents' 50th wedding anniversary. An item in the *Spokesman* on January 13, 1921, reported, "W. B. Curtiss is planning to begin the construction shortly of a five-room house on A Street opposite the present homes of L. S. Roberts and Denton G. Burdick." (Tonia Kissler Cain.)

From his arrival in Redmond in 1948 until his death in 2004, local pharmacist and businessman Vern Patrick was active in civic life in all capacities. In 1995, a new elementary school was named in his honor. The December 20, 1956, *Spokesman* noted, "Old St. Nick, who sometimes goes by the alias of Vernon Patrick . . . will be stationed near Cent-Wise Drugs, if youngsters still have Christmas wishes to whisper in his ear." (*Spokesman*.)

Arthur Tuck single-handedly won the state track meet for Redmond Union High School in 1919. The May 15, 1919, *Spokesman* reported, "Tuck . . . comes home loaded with Glory, Honor, Cups and Medals enough for a coat of mail. . . . He won in seven events and was second in one in which he made only a preliminary effort. In winning these seven events he established three new records for future comers to shoot at." Tuck was selected for the 1920 Olympic team and later joined the Oregon State Police. (*Spokesman*.)

Pictured at left in 1917, Anna Kissler models the doughboy uniform of a friend assigned to guard the Crooked River railroad bridge during World War I. Below, Curtiss and her mother, Elizabeth Kissler, show off fashions of the 1920s. Like many women of the day, Anna Curtiss played bridge. As the *Spokesman* noted on March 29, 1934, "Mrs. W. B. Curtiss entertained the Friendly Bridge Club Tuesday afternoon at her home on A Street. Honors were received by Mrs. O. E. Anderson, Mrs. Howard Hartley and Mrs. F. W. McCaffery." (Both Tonia Kissler Cain.)

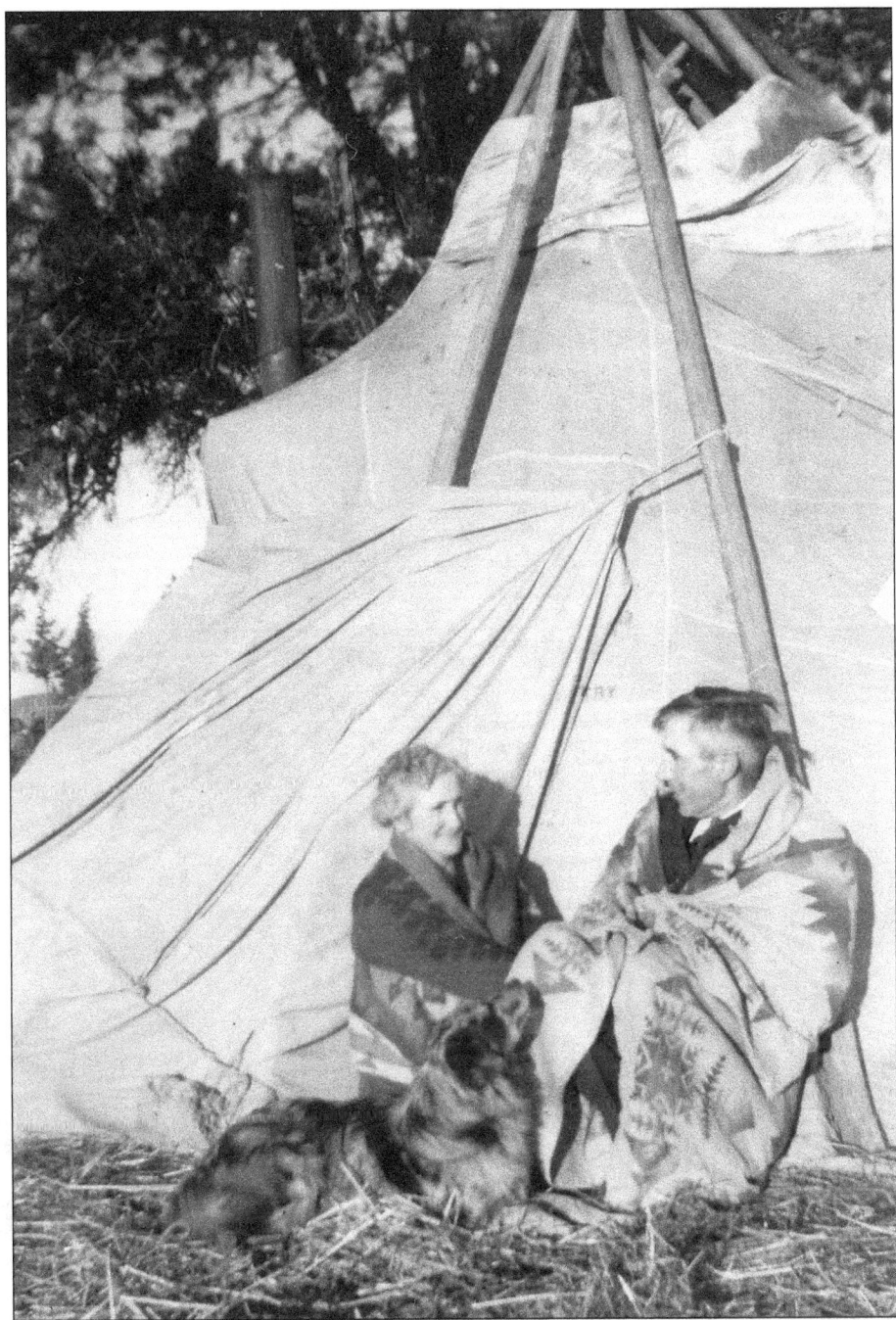

Pictured here from left to right, Arrista and Estell (E. E.) Burgess raised dairy cattle and potatoes on a farm in what is now northwest Redmond, where residents of the Warm Springs Reservation came to help with the harvest for many years. On December 7, 1939, the *Spokesman* reported, "Thirty friends gathered Monday evening to surprise Mr. and Mrs. E. E. Burgess on their thirtieth wedding anniversary. A mock wedding was held . . . Mr. and Mrs. Burgess were presented a lace tablecloth from the group. . . . The Burgesses have lived in this community for 19 years." (Penhollow family.)

A 1937 graduate of Redmond Union High School, Cal Butler was a key figure in Redmond's aeronautical history. After serving in the U.S. Army Air Corps during World War II, Butler returned to Central Oregon and opened a crop-dusting business. Later he promoted the use of air tankers to fight forest fires. The July 10, 1958, *Spokesman* read, "Despite the fact that his sprayer plane was minus its left landing gear, Pilot Cal Butler landed the aircraft with minor damage." (*Spokesman*.)

Former congressman Les AuCoin, third from left, was born in Portland but grew up in Redmond and graduated from Redmond Union High School in 1960. AuCoin represented Oregon's first congressional district in the U.S. House of Representatives for 18 years, ending in 1993. At age 32, he became the youngest house majority leader. On April 22, 1965, the *Spokesman* noted, "Les AuCoin, who is attending Pacific University at Forest Grove, came home Wednesday evening for a brief visit . . . AuCoin, member of the *Spokesman* staff last summer, is working part time in the sports department of the Portland Oregonian." (1958 RUHS yearbook.)

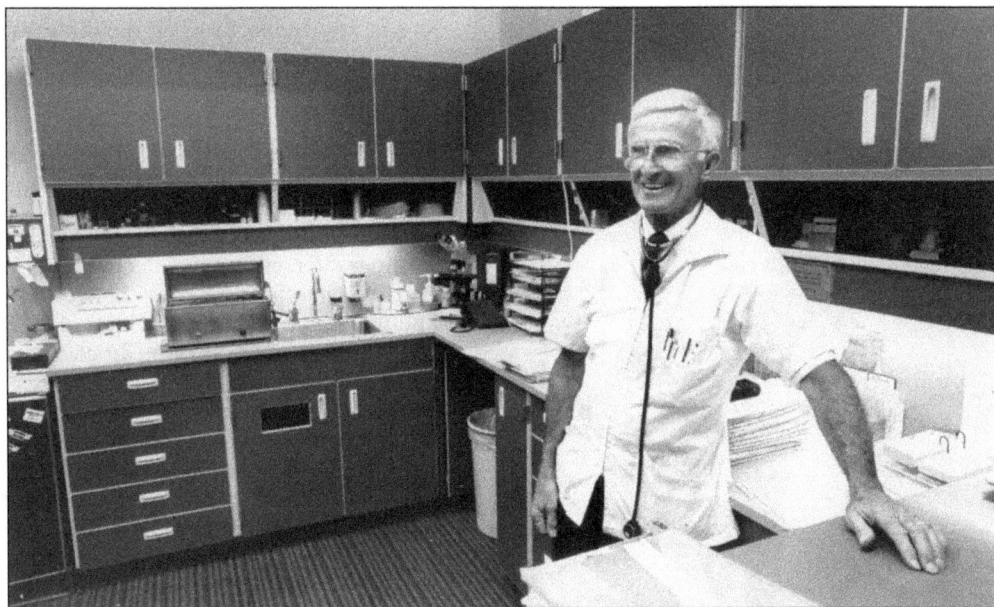

Longtime family physician Roger Stack came to Redmond in the early 1950s after his service during the Korean War in a MASH (Mobile Army Surgical Hospital) unit. Later his passion for green grass and trees led to his spearheading the planting of street trees downtown and the creation of a shady private park, which is now part of the city parks system. The March 11, 1981, *Spokesman* quoted Stack, "It's not really a park, but people can use it as long as they don't hurt the trees." (*Spokesman*.)

Lifelong Central Oregon rancher Howard Mayfield was an active Deschutes County Fair Association member for 37 years, giving so much to the event that in 1969 one day of the five-day-long county fair was named Howard Mayfield Day. Mayfield was also a Redmond city councilor. An August 6, 1969, *Spokesman* read, "Mayfield is humble about his long and successful service, considering whatever he has done as just a job that needed doing." (*Spokesman*.)

No one knows exactly when the Birdman began living in an old shack next to Cline Falls west of Redmond, perhaps in the late 1940s. There were even doubts about his real name—he was known as Abe Johnson and Charles Wheeler—but no one doubted his iconic status in the community. A hermit who lived without running water, electricity, or a job, the Birdman scavenged from the local landfill and relied on the kindness of strangers and friends. A 1969 article in the *Spokesman* brought the Birdman to the attention of the wider world, "It will seem like something out of a storybook when this kind gentleman calls the wild birds out of the surrounding trees and right into your hands." By the 1970s, the Birdman was entertaining children on field trips and had acquired a three-wheeled bike to get around. By the mid-1990s, ailing health forced the Birdman into a nursing home, where friends looked after him. (Both *Spokesman*.)

Grandson of pioneer settlers on the Deschutes River northwest of Redmond, Jess Tetherow was known throughout his life for his athleticism, especially on the baseball field. In April 1920, the *Spokesman* noted, "Jess Tetherow, for several years the leading pitcher of Central Oregon baseball, was present at the practice. . . . He will donate his services to help the Redmond team this year if a good team can be organized here." (Redmond Historical Commission.)

An itinerant photographer captured the Irvin women—Nell O'Dell Johnson Irvin, baby Grace, and Ruth, about 7 years old—in the living room of the family home at Northwest Seventh Street and Dogwood Avenue. As noted in the January 23, 1919, *Spokesman*, "A fine baby girl made her appearance at the home of Chad and Mrs. Irvin during the night of Jan. 22. Dr. Hosch and Miss Burgess were in attendance." (Ruth Ann Hartley.)

On November 6, 1985, the *Spokesman* ran this photograph of D. L. Penhollow at his last Lord's Acre Day as pastor of Powell Butte Christian Church. He retired after nearly 40 years as the church's pastor and founder of the church's popular fall fund-raising sale and barbecue. Penhollow came to Redmond as pastor of the First Christian Church and married local girl Marie Burgess. He got into politics during the 1960s, when he served on the Deschutes County Court (Commission). In Penhollow's retirement story, the *Spokesman* noted, "Weddings have been one of Penhollow's trademarks. He constantly is in demand to officiate at weddings and funerals. Since becoming a minister at Redmond First Christian Church in 1933, Penhollow has performed almost 2,800 weddings and officiated at almost 2,700 funerals." He died in 1986. (*Spokesman*.)

Four

EDUCATION

In the early decades of the last century, the area surrounding Redmond had many small, rural schools that serviced the farming communities in outlying areas such as Grey Butte, Cloverdale, Pleasant Ridge, and Lower Bridge. This Wilson School photograph is from about 1915. The December 23, 1915, *Spokesman* read, "A big rabbit drive was held Sunday in the Powell Butte district near the Wilson school house. . . . No guns were allowed at this drive." (Tonia Kissler Cain.)

Redmond's modern brick grade school opened in 1929, replacing a two-story wooden structure (above, at left) that had housed all grades. The old building was torn down after the new school opened. The brick building (below) served Redmond grade school students until 1995, when Vern Patrick Elementary opened. The building now is home to the Redmond Public Library. John Tuck, the grade school principal for many years, ran a tight ship. The *Spokesman* reported on September 30, 1934, "Thirty-five seconds after the gong sounded for fire drill at Redmond Grade School Monday, every pupil was out of the building. This is the quickest time ever made in fire drill, says John Tuck, grade principal, previous record time being 40 seconds. Fire drill is held frequently at the grade school, Tuck says, as a safety measure." (Above, Elizabeth Cockerham; below, Naomi Brown Mitchell.)

Redmond Grade School faculty poses outside their building in 1936. Principal John Tuck (front left) moved to Central Oregon from Arkansas and began teaching in the Cline Falls school after farming in Powell Butte briefly. He began teaching in Redmond in 1917; he served as principal of Redmond Grade School for 26 years. The upper elementary constructed in 1947 was named in his honor; it later became an elementary school. (Elizabeth Cockerham.)

The Redmond Grade School faculty poses here for this May 1947 photograph. Pictured from left to right are (first row) two unidentified, Elizabeth Cockerham, Dorothy Clapp, Margaret Thompson, two unidentified, Velma Brown, Blanche McFadden, and two unidentified; (second row) C. R. Lindsay, unidentified, Myrtle R., Mrs. Smith, Lillian Davis, Mary Thompson, unidentified, Jessie Hill, Irene Axtell, Archie Dunsmore, Clara Stacey, and Mr. Daugherty. (Elizabeth Cockerham.)

Jessie Hill (third row, center) taught first grade at Redmond Grade School from 1919 to 1948. The school was named in her honor when additional schools were built in 1948. This class is from 1934–1935. Hill was known for the kindness and support she gave her students and the birthday parties she gave for the children in her classes. (*Spokesman.*)

In this image of a classroom of first-graders at Redmond Grade School in 1945, Maude Gillmore is on the far left. Pupil George Taylor is marked with an X. A November 8, 1945, *Spokesman* stated, "The individual pictures taken early in the year of each student in the grade school have arrived and are now on sale in the office. Prices are as follows: one for 15 cents, three for 30 cents, six for 45 cents and the complete set for 65 cents." (Jessie Taylor.)

This is a class photograph for Jessie Hill Elementary School fifth-graders in 1960. Pictured from left to right are (first row) Quilcene Gordon, Vicki Allan, Tom Duval, Henry Gardner, Rita Sturza, Tommy Abbas, Susan Crockett, and Peggy Whitehead; (second row) Judy Boyer, Tonya Wyatt, Cathy Sala, Pamela Elskamp, Ralph Meeker, Fred Sutherland, Jean Green, Kathryn Forbes, Eugene Johnston, and Lloyd Murders; (third row) teacher Elizabeth Cockerham, David Smith, Gene Sloan, Larry Tull, Robbie Comstock, Dale Keller, Ronald Polly, Dennis Holmes, Tracy Steelhammer, Linda Sears, Nancy Donat, and Greg Westendorf. (Elizabeth Cockerham.)

This photograph is of the fifth-grade class at Jessie Hill Elementary School in 1964. From left to right are (first row) Florence Vail, Keren Addington, Veneta Olano, Sheila Petrie, Nancy Case, Vern Larrance, Dale Lehnertz, David Ladd, and Gary Lynch; (second row) Ray Taylor, Barry McCafferty, Joe Legg, Joyce Hartzell, Roger Saddoris, Connie Stivers, Mary Malick, Kirk Wright, Barbara Wainwright, and JoAnn Froelich; (third row) Phyllis Phillips, Jeff Givens, Clayton Ladrow, Debbie Greer, Jim Collell, Bradley Monical, Paul Morgan, Donna Devoe, Daryl Kemry, Terry Meyers, Bruce Cross, and teacher Elizabeth Cockerham. (Elizabeth Cockerham.)

Beginning in 1938, the high school played football in the Dry Canyon at a field built for that purpose initially called Juniper Bowl, then later Spud Bowl. In 1959, the Redmond Athletic Improvement League (RAIL) began efforts to build a new, bigger field near the old fairgrounds in southwest Redmond to be named Pollock Field in memoriam for a student. An August 25, 1960, *Spokesman* story on the new field stated, "With a gorgeous Central Oregon sunset as backdrop, dedication of the new James Pollock field was accomplished Friday evening under the lights with speaker paying tribute to the memory of the young athlete for whom the field was named." (Vernon Giles.)

The 1932 Powell Butte School football team beat Redmond 6-0 for the big game, with Harry Kissler scoring the only touchdown. The team, from left to right, included (first row) Robert Gessner, David Iverson, Clifford Montgomery, Robert Croon, Jack Vice, Clarence Kissler, and Glenn Ritter; (second row) Roy Moffett, Hoopity Miller, Floyd Kissler, Dick Minson, teacher Alby Beck, Homer Sleasman, Walt Kirby, Harry Kissler, and Oscar Smith. (Tonia Kissler Cain.)

Redmond junior and high school musicians traveled to the 1962 World's Fair in Seattle. Longtime band director Clyde Moore is in the second row on the far right. According to then eighth-grader Donna Scheel, the band had to raise money for the trip by putting on concerts in Redmond. The band performed at the World's Fair, and after that they were allowed to "go whole hog" touring the fair. (Donna Scheel Boehm.)

Every season, the Redmond High School football kickoff game day featured treats such as a picnic (with requisite games such as three-legged races) and a short parade downtown. In a September 16, 1967, story about the kickoff game, *Spokesman* writer Mickey Myrick commented, "What a massacre to Madras White Buffalos! Saturday was a builder upper for Redmond Panthers as they prepared for the Intermountain Conference opener at LaGrande Friday night. Cats got everything working at once Saturday afternoon and rolled over Buffs 47 to 0 in their second-straight league victory." (Both Vernon Giles.)

Construction of Redmond Union High School began in the spring of 1921. A *Spokesman* story on the dedication listed the new school's attributes: a study hall to seat 225; a home economics department with spacious accommodations for cooking and sewing, and a connecting cafeteria; an industrial arts department with the latest equipment——a mechanical drawing room, wood-working room, and finishing and forge room; agriculture, science, and commercial departments; four recitation rooms; office and board room; corridors large enough to accommodate steel lockers and added traffic from future additions to the building; two fireproof stairways; an electric program clock; and an electric fire alarm system and a telephone system. "Altogether it is a building . . . which should place it among the progressive institutions of our commonwealth," the *Spokesman* reported. In later years, the building would be used as a junior high, an educational center, and an elementary school. (Above, Tonia Kissler Cain; below, *Spokesman*.)

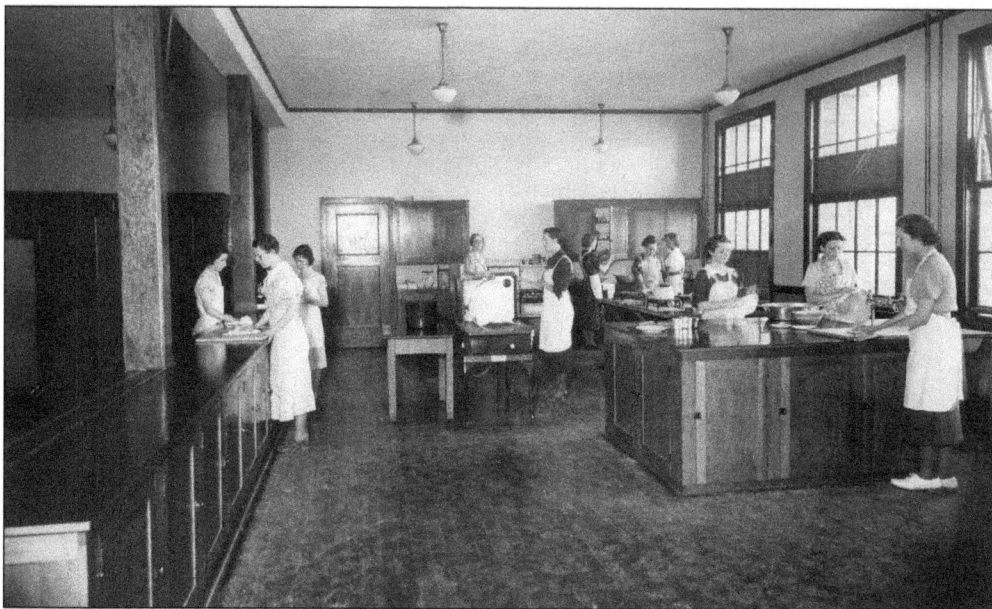

The high school's cooking classes often cooked and served meals to groups outside the classroom. The April 25, 1935, *Spokesman* stated that the "Foods Class, under the direction of Mrs. Orpha Benson, served a luncheon for grade school teachers Thursday." This photograph is from the same year. (*Spokesman*.)

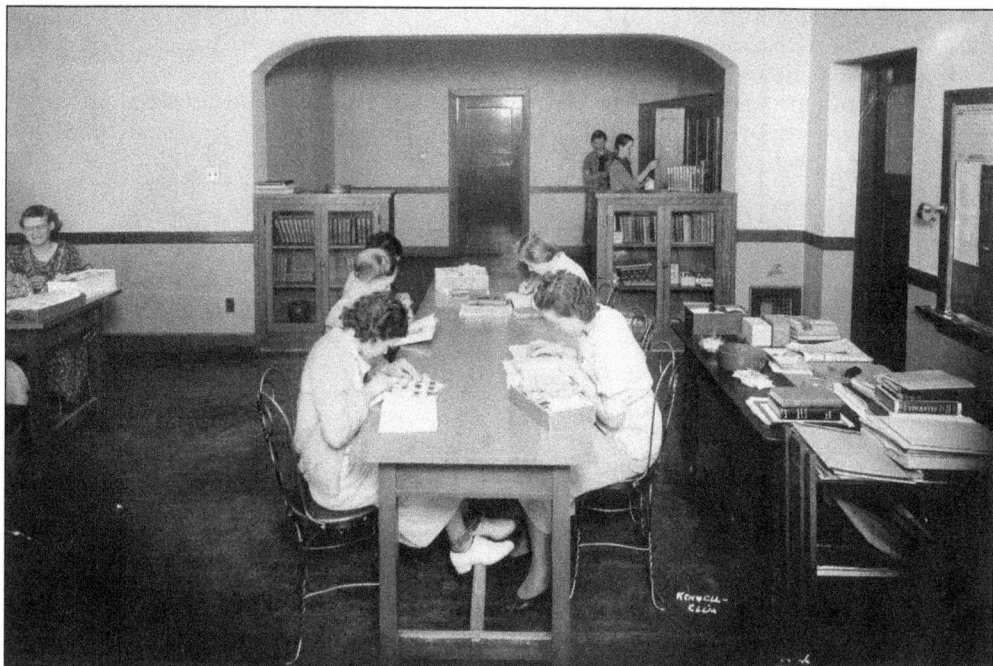

Redmond Union High School promoted the basics when it came to education: reading, writing, arithmetic, physical education, home economics, and career-building classes such as agriculture and business. On March 21, 1935, the *Spokesman* reported, "The state supervisor of home economics, Miss Bertha Kohlhagen, visited the Redmond [High School] department recently. She made brief talks about the advantages of studying home making." (*Spokesman*.)

Even today, Redmond High School is known for its vocational and technical programs in areas as diverse as aircraft mechanics, farming, and culinary arts. A September 11, 1966, *Spokesman* story stated, "Dennis Leon, 18, a graduate from Redmond Union High School, is the object of interest in the claims division of the State Compensation Department in Salem because he is the first male typist ever hired in the division." (1965 RUHS yearbook.)

In August 1957, Redmond honored Rex Putnam, Oregon's superintendent of public instruction, who had been superintendent of the Redmond schools for nine years, beginning in 1923. In May 1940, the *Spokesman* reported, "Rex Putnam of Salem, state superintendent of schools, stopped in Redmond Friday to visit friends. Putnam spoke at a meeting arranged by the Central Oregon League of Women Voters at the Pine Tavern in Bend Thursday evening." (Tonia Kissler Cain.)

Redmond Union High School's class of 1928 was the largest in its history at that point, with 36 graduates. The May 24, 1928, *Spokesman* story on the graduation stated, "The awards were popular with the audience and were a surprise to the students themselves, there being no advance information given out." (Tonia Kissler Cain.)

In the mid-1920s, a Redmond Union High School track relay team featured, from left to right, unidentified, Genevieve Cronin, Beulah Kissler, Vesta Partin, and Clara Peterson. Physical education classes were instituted in 1921, as the *Spokesman* noted on January 13, "Beginning next week a change in schedule at Redmond Union High School will provide physical training every day for both boy and girl students. The daily period for this work will be 20 minutes." (Tonia Kissler Cain.)

The Redmond Union High School graduating class of 1948 poses in two shots outside the school on Ninth Street. An advertisement aimed at graduating seniors ran in the May 20, 1948, *Spokesman* from the U.S. Army and Air Force, "The pay of a PFC is equivalent to civilian pay of $298.93 a month. Talk it over with the fellows in your nearest recruiting office—you probably know them." (Both Elton Lane.)

Transportation for a mostly rural school district could cause some problems. The August 4, 1932, *Spokesman* reported that voters in the high school district voted overwhelmingly to include $5,900 in the budget to provide transportation for high school students living more than 4 miles from the school. The publication stated, "The vote of 160 for and 77 against the measure indicated strong sentiment in favor of transportation of high school students." In the photograph above, Millie Elliott stands next to the Powell Butte bus on Ninth Street in front of Redmond Union High School in 1934. Below, the drivers from the 1947–1948 school year stand outside the school as well, including, from left to right, Chet Barbour, Marion Smith, Burton Brown, Al Prichard, and J. C. Line. (Above, Tonia Kissler Cain; below, Vernon Giles.)

Sisters Vivian and Masil Harrison pose around 1941 in front of the artillery piece that adorned the lawn at RUHS. The August 16, 1925, *Spokesman* reported that Redmond was to get a captured German fieldpiece, a 77-milimeter gun and carriage, suitable for mounting on a foundation near the flagpole at Redmond Union High School. The gun decorated the high school lawn until World War II, when it was donated to a scrap drive. (Vivian Harrison Campbell.)

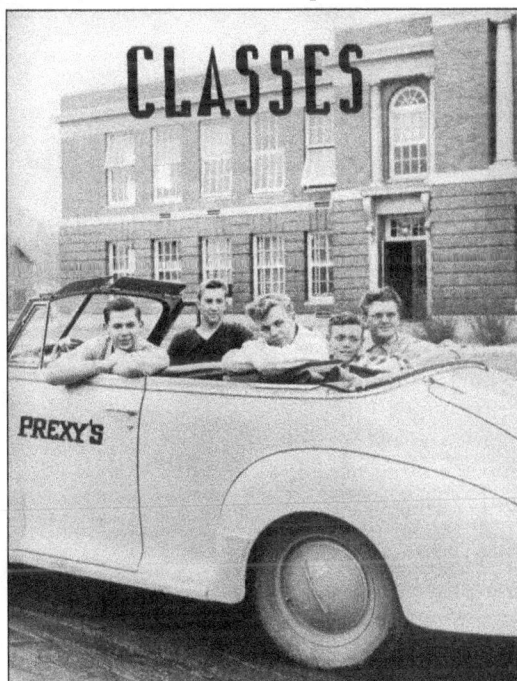

Redmond Union High School student government presidents in 1948 pose outside the school. From left to right are Phil Weigand, senior class president; Glenn St. Jean, vice president; Bud Henderson, junior class president; Ernie Magill, freshman class president; and unidentified. "Student body offices are almost exclusively held by seniors. Improvements in self-government this year are largely due to these officers' work in Panther Court, Panther Fangs, student council and student body meetings," stated the 1948 yearbook. (1948 RUHS yearbook.)

By the mid-1960s, when this photograph was taken, Redmond High School was getting dangerously overcrowded. A July 17, 1968, *Spokesman* article analyzing the state of schools in the district read, "How is the high school handling this problem? One way has been to rent classrooms near the main building, making possible five teaching stations to supplement the 31 in the high school." (Vernon Giles.)

The new Redmond High School, costing $3.2 million in 1970, featured many open classrooms, hoping to encourage a vibrant learning environment. (These were later walled off.) The school had a state-of-the-art public address system and featured hues of gold, orange, and brown. Graduates would later enjoy the ruse of convincing incoming freshmen that the concrete, windowless building was once a prison. (1971 RUHS yearbook.)

Five

CIVICS LESSON

The Redmond Kiwanis Club formed in October 1937 with 30 charter members. This photograph was assembled in 1938, when the club was filled with a variety of community leaders, from mill owners and managers to doctors, lawyers, and car dealers. Among them are drugstore owner Ernest C. Parker, Redmond mayor from 1935 to 1940, and attorney Virgil Langtry, who went on to serve on the Oregon Court of Appeals from 1969 to 1976. (Ruth Ann Hartley.)

Redmond has a long tradition of volunteerism and public service. The March 12, 1959, *Spokesman* reported, "Hugh Hartman and Vern Hassler received Redmond's 1958 distinguished service awards for leadership and service at Thursday's banquet in Westminster Hall." Hartman was a school principal and Hassler served as president of the Redmond Jaycee for 10 years; both were active in many other organizations. Pictured from left to right are Vern Hassler, Doris Hassler, Beatrice Hartman, and Hugh Hartman. (*Spokesman.*)

In June 1952, members of the junior high vacation church summer school took on the job of renovating the church bell from the 1911 First Methodist Church, which was destroyed by fire in January 1952. From left to right are (first row) Jud Van Gorter, Sharon Day, Fred Hirn, and Lynn Person; (second row) Ted Kromer, Dorothy Vilhauer, and Nancy Hartman; (third row) George Taylor, Norman Davis, and Randy Jones. (Jessie Taylor.)

The Deschutes County
Fair Board of Directors and
fairgrounds staff continue
to be important parts of
what make the regional
fair the top-attended event
in Oregon. This 1959
photograph was taken at
the fair rodeo grounds.
From left to right are (first
row) secretary Bill Hays,
Bud Adams, custodian
John Burns, and Wade
West; (second row) Carl
Galloway, Norm Swanson,
comanagers George
McKinnon and Roy
Newell, and president Roy
Carpenter. (*Spokesman*.)

A big part of every year's fair—especially for the hard working 4-H and FFA youth —is the annual
Kiwanis Livestock Auction. An August 4, 1966, *Spokesman*, stated, "The annual 4-H and FFA
market stock auction will kick off Friday evening. . . . Veteran auctioneers Jinks Tanler and Ross
Every, who each year donate their talents to this cause, will extol the virtues of each and every
animal for the edification and entertainment of prospective buyers." This photograph was taken
in the 1990s, before the fairgrounds were relocated. (*Spokesman*.)

Lord's Acre Day began just after World War II as a way to finance the building of the original brick structure for the Powell Butte Christian Church. The church congregation was encouraged to donate the harvest from 1 acre of farm ground. After the building effort was completed, a percentage of the proceeds from the event went to support church mission efforts. An October 30, 1968, *Spokesman* read, "The tangy smell of wood smoke and barbecued beef, the crisp cares of autumn breezes, the proliferate of politicians who speak only when spoken to, the wheedling banter of auctioneer Charlie Smith, happy people nodding to neighbors they see often and noisily greeting friends they haven't seen for a year, children squirming through the crowds, matrons leaving the country store with laden arms . . . these are the sights, smells, and sounds which set the Lord's Acre festival apart from other events." (*Spokesman.*)

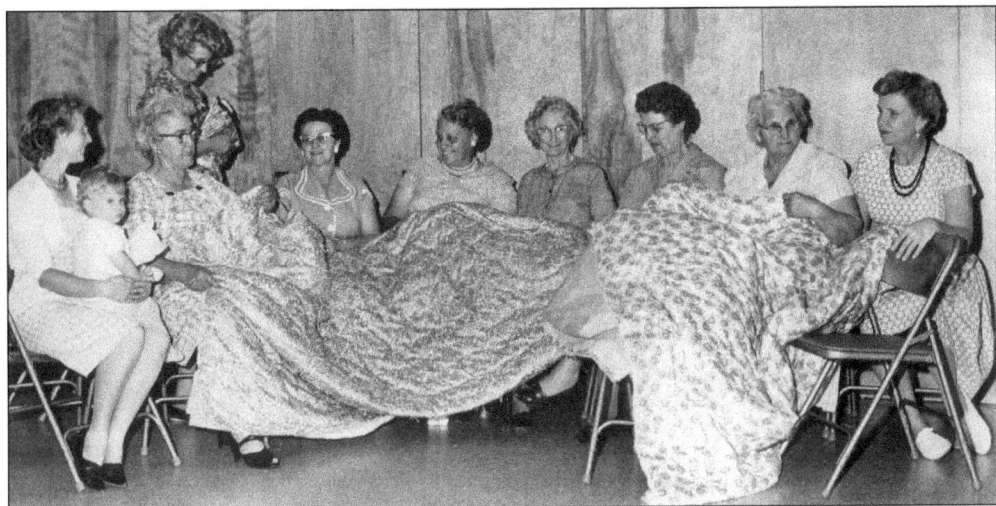

The undated photographs on these two pages, likely from the early 1960s, show all the activity associated with Lord's Acre: ladies working on a quilt for auction, folks eating pit barbecue lunches and homemade pie at the unique stand-up tables, and the fund-raising auction. Identified in the auction photograph from left to right are Gordon Fred Hall, Charlie Smith, Hoy Fultz, who is holding the quilt, and Don Cummings, to the lower right. (Both *Spokesman*.)

In 1941, members of the Redmond Volunteer Firefighter's Association formed a private social club, which was also open to retired firefighters. The group took its named from a Depression-era comic character, a whacky fireman named Smokey Stover. Its creator, Bill Holman, gave his blessing to the Order of Smokey Stover, which was a fixture in Redmond events and parades, such as the 1951 event above. Due to liability concerns, the group eventually discontinued its practice of conducting water fights along summer parade routes, as seen during the 1968 event below. A controversy about possible city subsidization of a private club where alcohol was served prompted the group to cancel its lease of the city-owned Smokey Hall building, and the club disbanded by the late 1990s. (Both Redmond Fire and Rescue.)

For most of its first half century, the Redmond Fire Department was largely comprised of volunteers. These firemen pictured above in 1949, in front of the fire hall, include Jack Parkey, captain of Company No. 2, who is lying down. An April 17, 1913, *Spokesman* read, "The drill nights are Tuesday and Friday at 7:15. Six slow taps of the fire bell is the signal for the firemen to assemble." On July 28, 1949, the *Spokesman* reported, "Harry Kissler, a member of the volunteer fire department, is dazed and shaken up but not seriously injured when he fell from a moving fire truck Monday evening. The accident happened during a fireman's speed drill near the railroad depot." (Above, *Spokesman*; below, Ruth Ann Hartley.)

During World War I, guards were posted at the Crooked River railroad bridge, as this photograph from 1917 shows. On July 18, 1918, the *Spokesman* stated, "The expense of guarding the Crooked River Bridge, here-to-fore borne by Deschutes County and amounting to about $500 per month, is to be borne by the state, as a result of a recent conference between H.H. DeArmond and Major Deich, commander of the state military police. The county will still furnish the rations and this should be defrayed jointly by Crook, Deschutes and Jefferson counties." (Both Tonia Kissler Cain.)

Townsfolk all did their part during World War II, such as these volunteers at Redmond Army Air Base fire station. An April 1, 1943, editorial titled "Temporary Situation" informed readers that raw sewage from Camp Abott upriver would continue to flow directly into the Deschutes River because of a lack of equipment available to provide an alternative. It commented, "As long as there is no other way out, however, it looks like central Oregon will have to grin and bear it and make another contribution to the war effort." (Redmond Historical Commission.)

A group of teenagers from Deschutes County were selected to travel to a national 4-H congress in 1958. From left to right are Pat Hollenbeck, Bend High School; Barbara Hansen, Bend; Keith Cyrus, Redmond Union High School; Jackie Jo Dick; and Ann Westfall, Bend. (*Spokesman*.)

Deschutes County celebrates a national 4-H club week every fall, often setting up exhibits for the public such as this undated one. A September 29, 1966, *Spokesman* read, "4-H has stolen the limelight this week . . . in many Redmond store windows. In observance of a 4-H week clubs are displaying everything from a shirt made by a boy in bachelor sewing, to a demonstration, complete with skeletons, of how to tell a horse's age by its teeth." (*Spokesman*.)

Mrs. Oswald Hanson, a 4-H foods club leader, helps David Perrin and brother Charles with bread contest practice in the summer of 1960. (*Spokesman*.)

A March 30, 1922, issue of the *Spokesman* contained a short snippet from its Powell Butte community notes, "Youngsters at the Wilson school have organized a calf club and will soon be in the game to beat Dad. County Agent Tucker will be the leader and the following have been chosen officers: Clara Brown, president (left); Gertrude Brown, vice-president (third from left); and June Chapman, secretary (second from right)." The club also had members Dorothy ?, second from left; Beulah Kissler, center; and Margaret Chapman, right. (Tonia Kissler Cain.)

Six

BUSINESS AND INDUSTRY

"Pay cash and pay less" was the motto of Howard Hartley's (right) grocery store on Sixth Street during the 1930s. His advertisements in the *Redmond Spokesman* always carried the tag "Trade where your dollar goes a long way but never leaves home." Among the store's specials the week of February 4, 1932, were Graham's Graham, the mush that is made in Central Oregon, at 10 pounds for 40¢, and Clearwater flour, a 49-pound sack for 89¢. (Ruth Ann Hartley.)

Clayton Downs grew good potato crops on his Powell Butte farm in the 1930s. His son-in-law Harry Kissler reportedly said the whole potato field was filled with spuds so big "you could stack them like cordwood on your arm." Throughout the decades when spud was king in the Redmond area, marketing efforts to make the world associate Central Oregon with Deschutes Netted Gem russet potatoes was a continuing effort. (Tonia Kissler Cain.)

Pickers for the potato harvest were a mix of migrant labor, workers from the Warm Springs Indian Reservation, and high school kids on break from Redmond High School, which often closed for a period during the harvest. During the harvest of 1948, students worked a total of 16,926 hours, or the equivalent of 2,686 six-hour days, filling 156,515 field sacks. This photograph, taken in the 1960s, depicts migrant pickers. (*Spokesman.*)

Spuds were still going strong in Central Oregon by the later half of the century, according to a February 12, 1969, *Spokesman* story, "Idaho came to Central Oregon last week to buy potatoes—the first time anyone can recall such a thing happening. Simplot, a large processing complex, bought 32,000 tons from two Madras growers." The same issue listed the cash produce buying prices for potatoes on the front page of the newspaper. (*Spokesman*.)

The first Netted Gem was planted in Central Oregon in the spring of 1909, and for a large part of the 20th century the Deschutes Netted Gem (the local name for the Russet Burbank variety) put areas around Redmond on the spud-growing map. Local potato production declined after irrigation projects led to large-scale farms in the Columbia Basin, and Central Oregon farmers could not compete. (*Spokesman*.)

Here Winnie Mae Youngs Woodward plows her garden on the family farm west of Juniper Butte near Culver in the mid-1940s. Farmers north of Redmond greatly benefited from the completion of the North Unit irrigation project in 1946. The day the water was turned on, May 18, was one of celebration for the area; water began flowing to the first 15,000 to 20,000 acres between the Crooked River Gorge and Agency Plains near Madras. (Woody Woodward.)

Dryland wheat was the cash crop of choice among the area's earliest farmers, especially those in the Lamonta and Culver areas, such as the Rodman Ranch pictured here at harvest in 1910. The July 20, 1911, *Spokesman* noted, "Owing to the Redmond District being located in the center of the largest irrigated section of Oregon, there is no danger of any crop failure no matter how hot the weather gets." (Redmond Historical Commission.)

A hay wagon at the Kissler farm in Powell Butte around 1925 takes feed to livestock during a snowstorm. Winter temperatures far below zero were more typical in the 20th century. On February 9, 1933, the *Redmond Spokesman* reported, "Redmond was one of Central Oregon's warm spots last night with a minimum temperature of 24 degrees below zero." (Tonia Kissler Cain.)

Cows lounge on the Burk dairy farm north of Redmond around 1995. The dairy industry flourished in Central Oregon until late in the 20th century. An item in the June 23, 1914, *Spokesman* reported, "The Redmond Creamery is now shipping out weekly about 2,000 pounds of high grade butter to Portland and other towns along the railroad." By January 1941, the Central Oregon Dairy Herd Improvement Association boasted 44 members. (*Spokesman*.)

On August 10, 1911, the newspaper read, "Call up the *Spokesman* if you have any news that is news, the *Spokesman* would like to print it. If you are going out of town or away on a visit, if you have relatives or friends visiting you, if you know of any one sick. . . . Use the phone liberally and let us have the news happenings in your neighborhood." The *Redmond Spokesman* printed its first issue on July 14, 1910, a week after Redmond became an incorporated city. H. H. and C. L. Palmer (Henry and Clara) moved their newspaper plant to Redmond from Laidlaw (now Tumalo). In July 1914, the *Spokesman* bought the *Oregon Hub*, which had set up shop in Redmond in 1909, and the year-old *Enterprise*. In the mid-1960s, production manager Jim Sage gave the Redmond High School journalism class a tour of the newspaper office and printing press. (*Spokesman*.)

Over the next 15 years, the *Spokesman* went through three publishers—M. W. Pettigrew, Douglas Mullarkey, and Edgar Bloom—until Joe and Mary Brown bought the business in 1931. After their divorce in 1955, Mary Brown continued to own and operate the business until selling it to Western Communications in 1971. In June 1939, the *Spokesman* moved into a new custom-built office at 321 Southwest Sixth Street. On June 8, just before the move, the *Spokesman* commented, "The architects say the entrance is of fluorescent glass in pylon effect. Townspeople, however, describe it as a glass chimney surmounting a stack of Pyrex dishes." When Western Communications purchased the newspaper, its offices moved to the former showroom of a plumbing shop at 226 Northwest Sixth Street, while Brown kept the brick building for her printing business. (*Spokesman*.)

In 1928, a three-story brick building rose from the ashes of the wood-framed Redmond Hotel that had burned along with surrounding businesses in June 1927. The new establishment, now called New Redmond Hotel, was the height of modern sophistication. "Luxury, beauty, comfort and convenience—all are combined in this magnificent structure, the forerunner of greater progress for Redmond," touted a full-page advertisement for the hotel in the July 26, 1928, *Spokesman*. (Both *Spokesman*.)

Present Mortuary and Ambulance
cost 2200⁰⁰ no debt

Above, a new mortuary van and ambulance sits at the 300 block of Southwest Seventh Street in front of Chad Irvin's mortuary. Chad Irvin placed the following advertisement in the May 10, 1934, *Spokesman*, "We bury the just and the unjust—the transient with 2 cents and a package of cigarette papers in his pocket." The photograph below, from October 1939, shows construction of the Chadwick building at Southwest Seventh Street and Deschutes Avenue. An advertisement in the April 25, 1940, *Spokesman* announced, "We will be known as the Irvin Chapel Mortuary—and will soon be working in our new building. This entire country tried to build a hospital and couldn't do it. I have built an institution with my own money and a loan on my own property and what I have done for the community as well as myself would, when finished, build that hospital and equip it." (Both Ruth Ann Hartley.)

Congratulations FROM THE MANAGEMENT
AND EMPLOYEES OF GREAT LAKES CARBON

Great Lakes Carbon was just one of the companies that operated the diatomite mine at Lower Bridge over the years. In August 1919, the *Spokesman* reported, "The Western Diatomite concern is doubling the capacity of its plant near Lower Bridge in order to handle the greatly increased demand for its products. Manager Bruce has made a proposition to the county court to join in the improvements of the road between the plant and Terrebonne, which is the shipping point." (1958 RUHS yearbook.)

The Tite Knot Pine Mill, pictured here in 1949, was one of several that called Redmond home, beginning in the 1930s and continuing into the 1990s. On October 2, 1947, the *Spokesman* noted, "Tite Knot cuts about two and a half million board feet of lumber per month in its Redmond plant, operating two shifts with some 60 men employed in the mill here." (Redmond Historical Commission.)

In August 1963, Tite Knot Pine was destroyed by fire. Firefighters were hampered by a lack of water, and the event prompted city officials and voters to approve upgrades to the city's water system. The August 8, 1963, *Spokesman* reported, "Approximately 125 men have been employed in the mill at Redmond and another 50 in logging operations. Tite Knot furnishes Redmond's largest payroll, this having amounted to $638,486.49 in 1962." (Redmond Fire and Rescue.)

C. H. "Chad" Irvin stands in his furniture store on Sixth Street in 1911 (above) and in November 1931 (below). His businesses grew to include a mortuary, as people ordered coffins from the furniture store. In 1912, Irvin moved from a wood-framed building to a new one constructed of tuff stone at 421 Southwest Sixth Street. The March 21, 1912, *Spokesman* commented, "The first stone building in Redmond to be built with lava rock was the Chad Irvin store on Sixth Street and this has been succeeded by the August Anderson building on South Sixth Street, between E and F streets. . . . Practically, the building problem in this section has been solved, and it will not be long before Redmond will be known as the city of stone buildings, both in the business and residence districts." (Both Ruth Ann Hartley.)

Safeway came to Redmond in 1931, and in 1940 its first new store was built. The structure later housed city hall. The December 10, 1940, *Spokesman* reported, "Newest addition to Redmond's business life, the huge Safeway Stores' super-market erected at a cost of about $20,000 on the corner of Seventh and E streets, will open for business Friday morning. . . . Customers will find wide, spacious aisles, new eye-level displays with a new design in shelving and the latest methods of food handling." (*Spokesman.*)

Lester Taylor Jr. (far right) and his coworkers get ready for a sale at Piggly Wiggly in 1965. In 1939, the market built its new store. As the *Spokesman* reported on September 28, 1939, "Piggly Wiggly will construct one of the most modern stores in the Northwest, a super drive-in market of the latest type, on the four lots on Sixth Street between Galloway's and the Kendall building, announces Ned Fields, manager." (Lester Taylor Jr.)

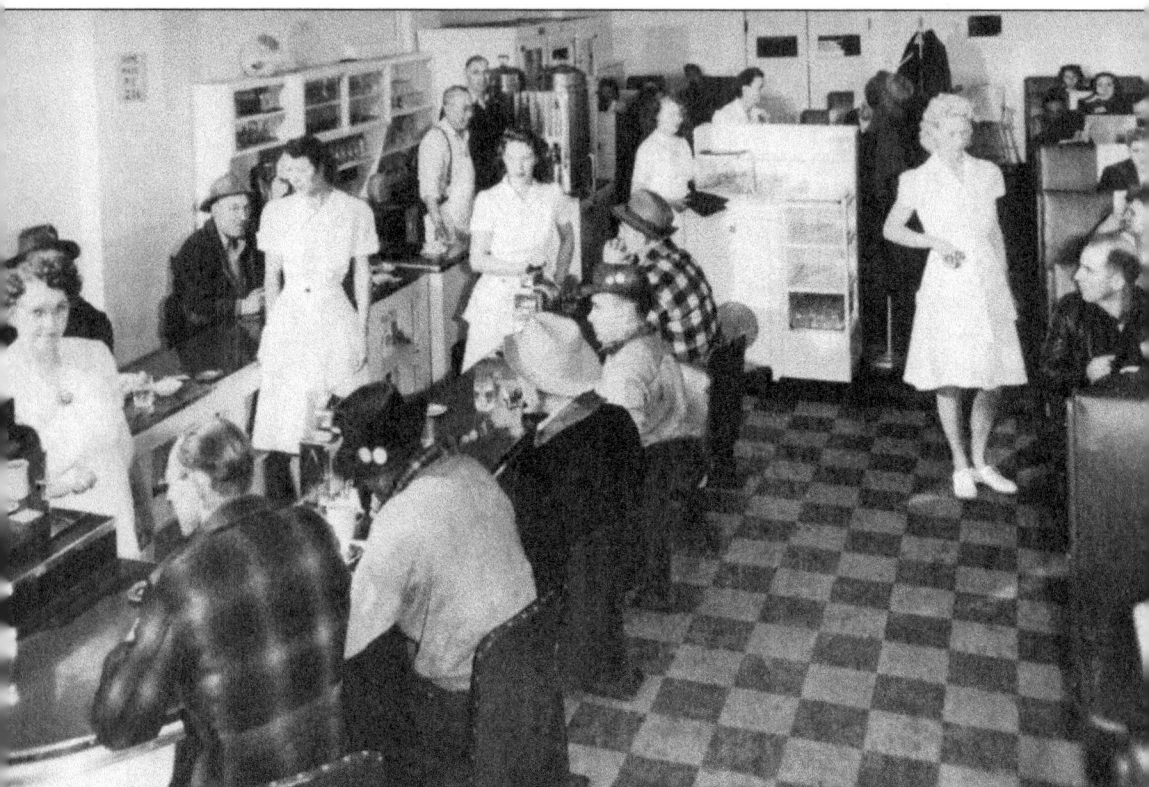

In 1949, Stockton's Café was owned by George Howe and Elvis Stockton, but pictured standing in the back left with the white apron is cook Johnny Young, future owner of Stockton's. Young was an immigrant from Canton, China, who began living in Redmond after World War II. A 1960 advertisement bragged, "Come to Stockton's for Chinese foods; orders to go, if you wish. American Foods—the best in eating!" (1949 RUHS yearbook.)

In the postwar years, Redmond had multiple barbershops, many downtown. In Redmond Union High School's 1948 yearbook, the Redmond Barbershop bragged on its "Really good fountain service and lunches, magazines and ice. . . . We trim you good!" (1948 RUHS yearbook.)

Redmond's Dairy Queen, pictured here in the mid-1960s, has been located on south Sixth Street for more than 50 years. An October 22, 1969, *Spokesman* story about the construction of a new addition, according to owner Everett Reynolds, stated, "The addition will be heated in the winter and air conditioned in the summer, with no more table service." (*Spokesman*.)

The dominant retail force in Redmond until the latter half of the 20th century, Lynch and Roberts opened in 1910. In 1946, the partners divided up the sales area. J. R. and Maurice Roberts took the groceries and dry goods as well as ladies wear, and M. A. Lynch had clothing for men and boys. (*Spokesman.*)

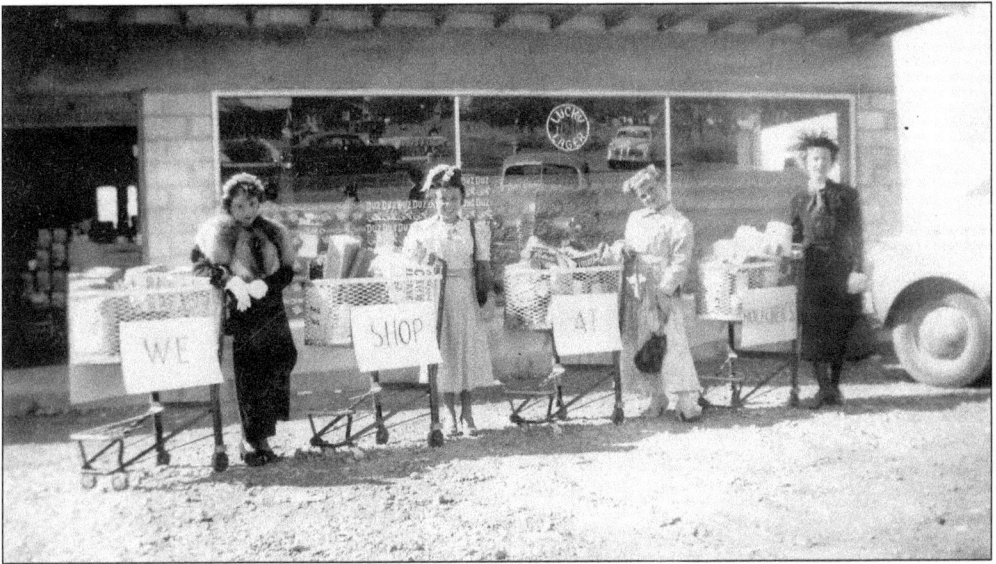

Here Retha Holechek and friends gather at Holechek Market on Highland Avenue to prepare for a parade in the 1950s. In true small-town tradition, Redmond parades are liberally sprinkled with entries highlighting local businesses. (Holechek family.)

In 1948, Dahl's Drugs was located at 447 Southwest Sixth Street. A 1948 Christmas advertisement from the *Spokesman* states, "The true meaning of friendship has been brought home to us very clearly during the these last weeks as a result of the fire damage which necessitated closing our store until it could be repaired and new stock obtained. . . . We're back in business now, ready to serve you." (*Spokesman.*)

Today's Sno-Cap Drive-In started in the mid-1950s as Peden's Ice Cream. George Trout (left) and son Rick Trout (right) flank employee Donna Scheel in this photograph from the early 1960s. At the time, the shop and the Hub Motel across the highway were on the northern fringe of Redmond. On November 21, 1963, the *Spokesman* reported, "George and Eileen Trout are the new owners of Peden's Ice Cream. They opened this week with Joe and Maxine Peden helping the Trouts for a while. Last year the Trouts operated the Sno-Cap ice cream shop in Sisters." (Donna Scheel Boehm.)

Bob and Ula Blair's Brand restaurant was a fixture in Redmond for many years, both in its original location downtown and later south of town. The July 11, 1963, *Spokesman* reported the last move, "Featured, of course, are Blair's 1,200 or more authentic brands, which he collected from all over Oregon, as well as other localities. . . . The Blairs sold their former downtown Brand Café, now the Frontier Café, last May to Bruce and Alice Johnson." (*Spokesman*.)

The June 30, 1927, *Spokesman* reported, "$750,000 fire destroys two business corners. A Tuesday morning fire destroyed a large area of business places on Sixth Street. The alarm brought Redmond citizens out of bed at about 3 o'clock to find to the old Oregon Hotel a mass of flames." The fire destroyed most of the buildings on both sides of Sixth Street, between Evergreen and Forest Avenues. (Ruth Ann Hartley.)

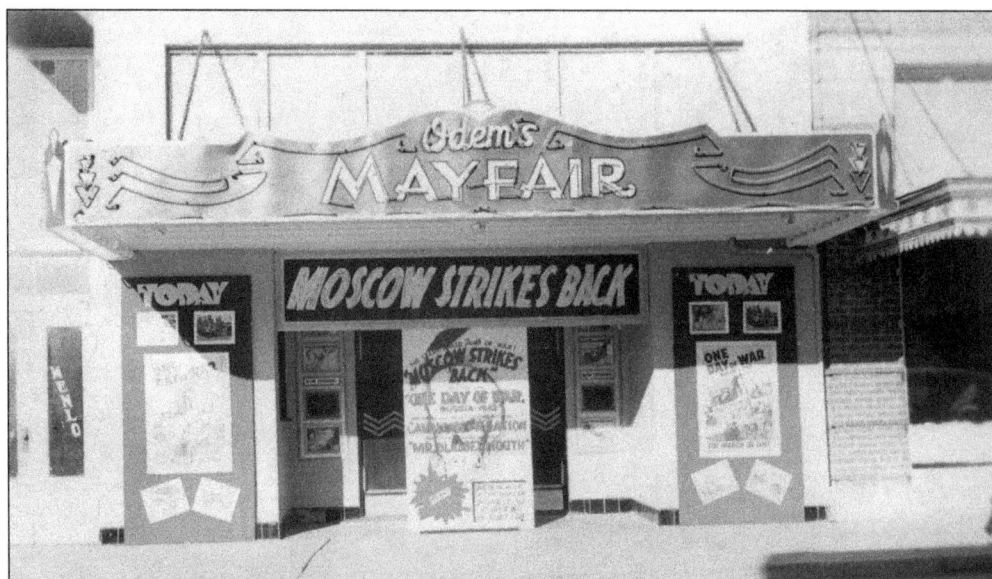

Milt and Flossie Odem came to Redmond in 1929, and for the next three decades they owned local movie theaters—two downtown and a drive-in south of town. As the *Spokesman* reported on May 24, 1934, "Work of installing new seats in the Hiway theatre will be completed in time for the show Friday night, after a shut-down of two days this week. . . . The new seats are the most comfortable and up-to-date on the market, says Milt Odem, theatre manager. The old ones, with plain wood, were not cut to fit the slope of the floor and echoed sound. The new ones are upholstered in leather." The Hiway Theater on Southwest Sixth Street became the Mayfair, shown in this photograph from 1943. The family also opened a drive-in theater in 1952 between South Highway 97 and South Canal Boulevard, where the current Redmond Theater currently sits. (Above, Bob Brown; below, *Spokesman*.)

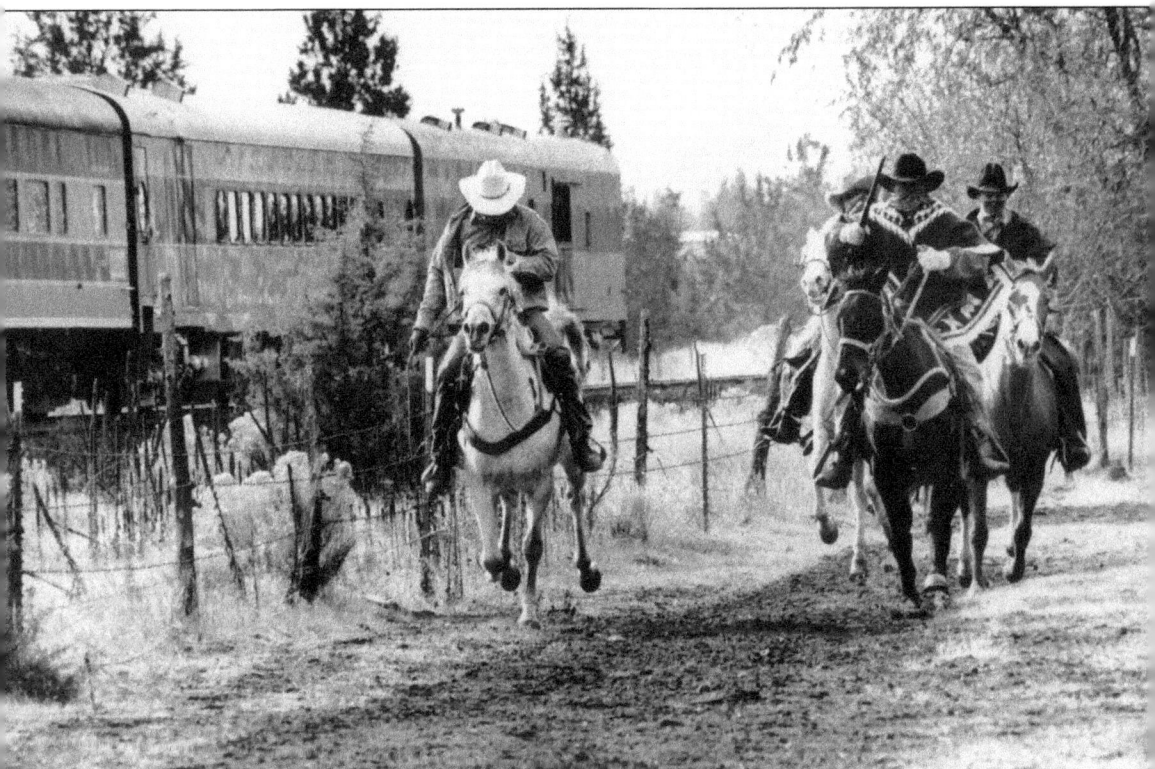

The Crooked River Dinner Train—part theater, part restaurant, part old-fashioned jaunt on the rails—opened in 1991, its station located at O'Neil Junction north of Redmond. As the region entered the 1990s, tourism became a focus for those looking to replace the diminishing industries of wood products, farming, and ranching. In 1994, Central Oregon received a $770,000 grant to build up its tourism and technology sectors. Tourism can be a fickle thing to rely on, however; in 2004, the city of Prineville purchased the dinner train, hoping to capitalize on its existing ownership of the rail line. But in 2008, the dinner train was closed due to declining ridership. By early 2009, a private owner stepped forward to renew the dinner train in the midst of uncertain economic times. (*Spokesman.*)

In 1967, Vern Patrick, owner of Cent-Wise Drugs, bought the Franks building that he had leased since 1953. The *Spokesman* reported that the site had a long history, with the original deed from December 2, 1905, belonging to B. S. Cook. In 1905, taxes on the lots were $8.55 and in 1920, $82.68. By 1967, they had risen to about $11,000, the *Spokesman* reported. (*Spokesman*.)

Seven

JUST FOR FUN

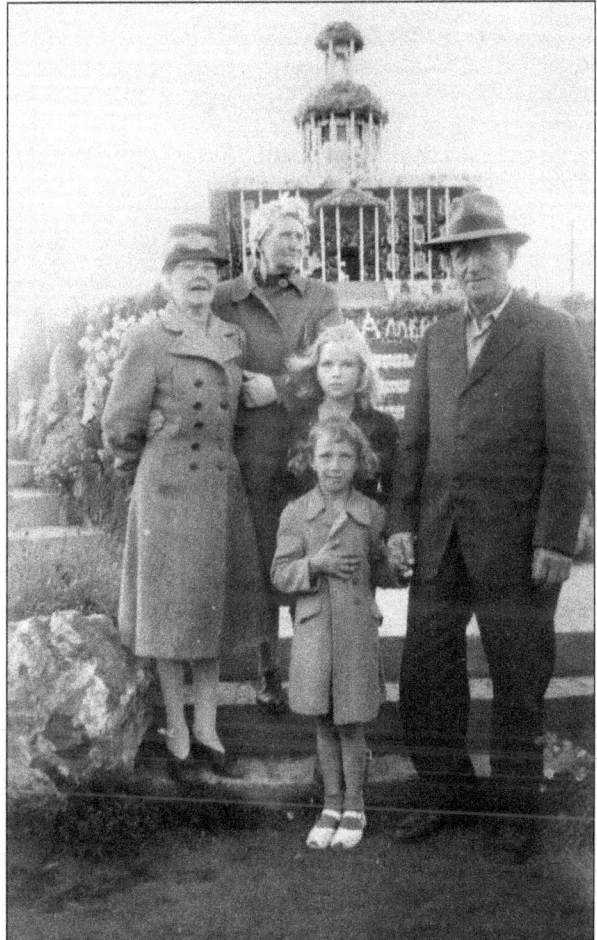

Not even the Petersen family descendents remember exactly when farmer Rasmus Petersen's backyard landscaping project turned into a full-fledged roadside attraction. But somewhere along the way, the acres of elaborate rock building, bridges, and castles, surrounded by moats, peacocks, and fountains, became a must-see Redmond destination. Visiting the gardens in this 1947 photograph are, from left to right, (front) Margit Petersen and Carl Hansen; (back) Margarite Scott, Carrie Hansen, and Lois Petersen. (Lois Frey.)

Redmond and rodeo have gone together since the beginning, when the first cowboy felt compelled to show off in the corral for his friends. A 1935 *Spokesman* story read, "Most spectacular rodeo event was the wild buffalo ride by Norman Jones. After a successful ride, he got tangled in a lariat and the buffalo dragged him down the track. He was saved by the expert riding and roping of Alf Parkey." (*Spokesman.*)

For a few heady years, Redmond hosted an air show at Roberts Field, hoping to make it an annual event. Nearly 45,000 people showed up for the inaugural event in June 1988 to watch the action. The June 22, 1988, *Spokesman* stated, "Several people suffered heat exhaustion, keeping ambulance crews busy. Redmond Fire Department cooled some willing spectators who ventured under the spray of a fire hose." The event died out by the mid-1990s. (*Spokesman.*)

Known to locals not by its proper name, Operation Santa Claus, but as the Reindeer Ranch, this 50-plus-year establishment has been entertaining children in the high desert for decades. Local rancher John Zumstein spent years importing reindeer and learning to acclimate them to the unusual surroundings. His ranch on Helmholtz Way, west of Redmond, was open year-round and featured a suited Santa and sleigh for souvenir photographs. The reindeer participated in the Redmond holiday parade and were often walked around downtown to delight the youngsters. Beginning in 2002, Santa's herd fell under traveling restrictions meant to curtail Chronic Wasting Disease, an epidemic among deer and elk in many regions, diminishing the visibility of the business. (Stranahan family.)

For much of its history, the Deschutes County Fair ended its weekend with an early Sunday morning feast, the Buckaroo Breakfast. The September 12, 1946, *Spokesman* reported, "Brahma bulls and bucking horses began arriving in Redmond this week, banners went up in the streets and store fronts . . . breakfast cooks have sharpened their knives and now for the twenty-seventh successive year the final careening week of preparation for the Deschutes County Fair is at hand." (*Spokesman.*)

A tradition that began in 1944 and is forever linked with the last Sunday of the Deschutes County Fair, the Buckaroo Breakfast was described in a 1967 letter to the *Spokesman* from an impressed visitor from the Willamette Valley, "There are 16 pumice brick fireplaces in a double row inside a semi-circle of tables. There are two steak stoves, two bacon stoves and so on and each club member has a stove or station for which he assumes responsibility, and gets his own crew. Most unique was the long fire trench where the pan bread was cooked." Quantities of food that year were 2,900 steaks, 200 half-pints of milk, 484 dozen eggs, 550 pounds of bacon, and 1,000 pounds of potatoes. (Both *Spokesman.*)

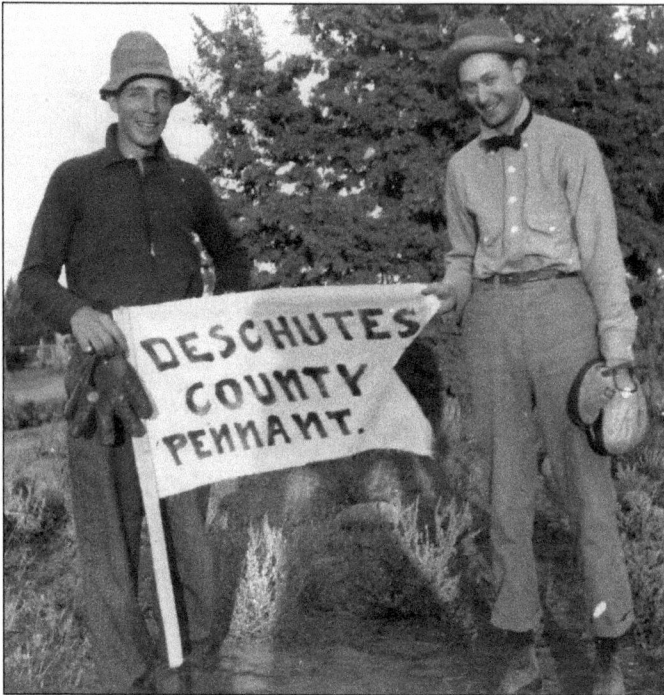

J. R. Roberts (right) and an unidentified teammate help show off a winning pennant from early in the 20th century. Baseball was a part of community life. The town team played teams from other Central Oregon communities, teams of Redmond bachelors took on Redmond married men, and thin commercial club members played their heftier counterparts, all providing great Sunday afternoon entertainment. (Redmond Historical Commission.)

Leo Davis (back right), then sports editor for the *Spokesman* (and future *Oregonian* writer), poses in this photograph with one of Redmond's community baseball teams sometime in the early 1950s. The team included, from left to right, (first row) Bud Van Matre, Harley Hart, Harold Povey, Jack Hassler, Marv Scott, Ray Douglas, Vern Hassler, and Hank Cooper; (second row) George Taylor, Riley Sanders, Jim Griffith, and Davis. (George Taylor.)

The Potato Show was the precursor to the county fair, featuring prizes for other agricultural products and livestock raised in the region, but it highlighted potatoes, a crop Central Oregon was quickly becoming known for. An October 3, 1912, *Spokesman* article stated, "Free band concerts will be given each evening of the show, and visitors to the city will be entertained in the free, open-hearted manner for which the Redmond people are famous." This 1911 photograph was taken at the time of the second annual Potato Show. Pictured from left to right are Fred Stanley, president of irrigation company; William Buckley, freighter; George Rodman, banker; Kirk Whited, farmer; Bob McSherry, lumber company owner; and Bill McSherry, feed store owner. (*Spokesman.*)

The Potato Show was renewed in 1958 with a renamed Redmond Potato Festival that was celebrated every September. An article from the June 26, 1958, *Spokesman* read, "Redmond's forthcoming Potato Festival, Sept. 20, should remind old-timers of a similar celebration Nov. 2, 1911. When Redmond had its first 'Potato Day' 47 years ago, even residents of the district were astounded at the variety and excellence and large yields. . . . In 1911 russets were known as Netted Gems and shared the spotlight with Irish Cobbler, Uncle Sam, Gold Coin, Hundred Fold, Burbank, Early Ohio, Peerless, Early Rose and Gold Dollar varieties." This undated photograph was taken on Deschutes Avenue. The Potato Festival continued until 1970. (*Spokesman.*)

During the festival, a king and queen were chosen from amongst the farming royalty in the Redmond area. The couple reigned over a court of spud princesses, such as this 1958 trio, from left to right, of Corleen Kraft, Pat McClure, and Judy Lisius. Not pictured is Sue Swearingen, Miss Spud for 1958. The 1958 Potato Festival King George Elliott and Queen Mary Mustard (below) had each been farming potatoes for nearly 50 years. (Both *Spokesman*.)

For decades, everything was spud in Redmond, even this Spudnik float in 1958. A September 15, 1966, *Spokesman* reminded shoppers that potato sack vests were still available for purchase at local clothing stores. "The lined and trimmed vests were made from potato sacks by Cascade Home Extension Unit members." (*Spokesman.*)

By 1970, the potato industry had begun to diminish, and the Potato Festival was losing steam. This photograph of the barbecue beef pit was taken on Seventh Street in Redmond in September 1969, one year before the festival celebrated with a swan song. (*Spokesman.*)

Redmond's police force joined in donning Old West attire during the celebration of Oregon's centennial in 1959. Standing in front of the police station at Southwest Seventh Street and Evergreen Avenue, from left to right, are Leonard Kirby, Bob Kent, Speed Durgan, Chief Mel Mooney, and Bob Dickerson. (*Spokesman.*)

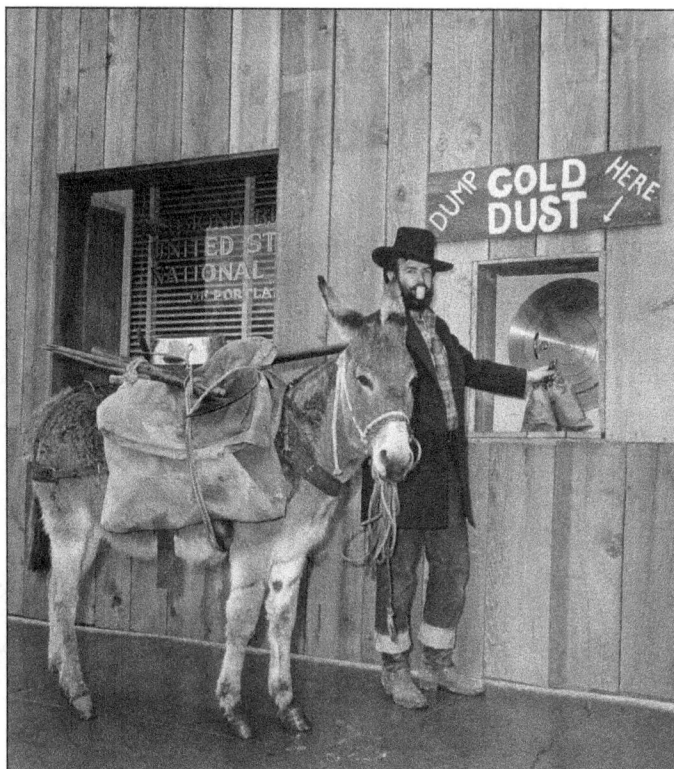

Redmond went all-out to celebrate Oregon's centennial in 1959. In addition to issuing commemorative coins and encouraging period dress, downtown businesses put up false fronts and called the town Juniper Junction. Jake Ledbetter makes a deposit with Honky the donkey (owned by Rusty Modrell) at Redmond's U.S. National Bank. (*Spokesman.*)

In honor of Oregon's centennial in 1959, pictured from left to right, Eileen Trout, Donny Trout, and Rova Galloway show off items from Mrs. Galloway's vintage clothing collection outside the *Spokesman* office. Her costume was 100 years old. The suit worn by Mrs. Trout once belonged to Mrs. Galloway's aunt, and Donny Trout sported an outfit once worn by Jess Butler. (*Spokesman.*)

In May 1959, the Deschutes County Cattlemen's Association organized an old-fashioned cattle drive through downtown Redmond as part of the celebration of Oregon's statehood centennial. The *Spokesman* reported that more than 200 animals took part. (Lloyd Meeker.)

In 1985, both the *Spokesman* and the city of Redmond celebrated 75 years of existence during the Fourth of July festivities. Longtime *Spokesman* employees Martha Stranahan (left) and Mickey Myrick ride on the parade float during the Independence Day parade downtown. (*Spokesman*.)

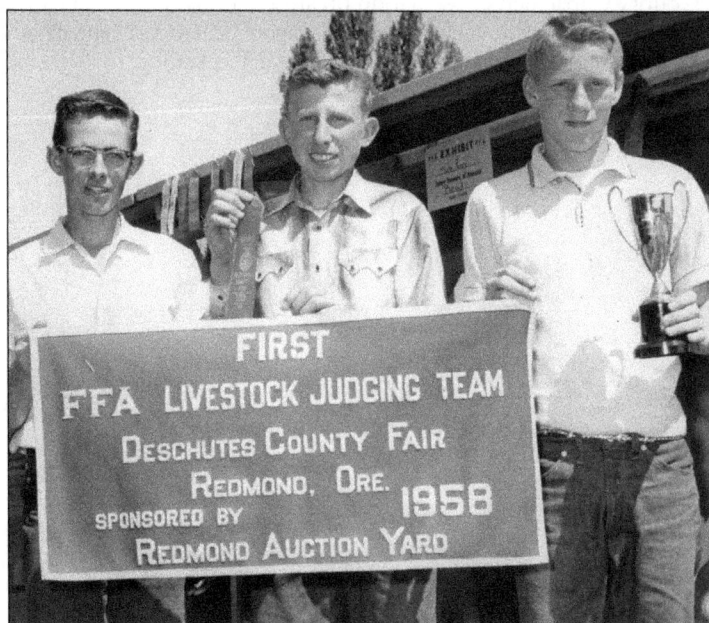

These Future Farmers of America winners are unidentified, however FFA and 4-H participation has always been high in Redmond. The August 27, 1959, *Spokesman* stated, "Portable stall space has been added at the fairgrounds this year to accommodate an expected increase in 4-H, FFA and open class entries. There will be lights strung along the livestock barns for the convenience of visitors in the evening and show rings are turfed this year." (*Spokesman*.)

Unidentified volunteers help process entries for open class at the Deschutes County Fair in this late-1950s photograph. The July 21, 1966, *Spokesman* read, "Open class entries are still being accepted, according to County Extension Agent Jane Schroeder. . . . To avoid the rush of that day, they may drop by the fairgrounds before that time and pre-enter. This will . . . eliminate long lines." Open class categories included ceramics, photography, needlework, foods and canning, and floral exhibits. (*Spokesman.*)

The August 27, 1959, *Spokesman* declared the fair's 4-H horse day winners, from left to right, as Jane Kasserman, Kay Asselin, Cathie Lanthorn, Mary Dorsch, and Nina West. It went on to state, "Cathy Lanthorn, queen of Deschutes County Fair, won a prized honor Tuesday afternoon, adding to laurels gained in 4-H horsemanship and showmanship contests. She accomplished all 14 movements required for the 4-H senior horsemanship award, better known to yearning young riders as the Dad Potter competition." (*Spokesman.*)

Lena Hartley (far left) dances while her daughter Ruth Hartley Doudiet snaps a photograph. For many years, residents of the Warm Springs Indian Reservation were an important part of the Redmond community. Warm Springs families formed close bonds with farmers, as they worked harvests together year after year. Redmond town teams played Warm Springs teams in baseball, basketball, and football, and Warm Springs residents were a big part of the Deschutes County Fair, from their encampments to participation in rodeo and horse racing. The building on the old fairgrounds that housed the textile exhibits was named for Lucy Miller, a member of the tribes who encouraged Warm Springs women to enter exhibits. In its coverage of the 1932 fair, the *Spokesman* noted, "Little Alec Henries of Warm Springs was the youngest person at the Deschutes County Fair. He was born in the Indian encampment at the fair." (Ruth Ann Hartley.)

The Downs children of Powell Butte are in costume for Halloween in 1920. Pictured from left to right are Lloyd, Leonard, and Margaret Downs. From 1937 until the early 1960s, Neewollah parades kept kids busy on Halloween. As the *Spokesman* reported in October 1939, "Purpose of the parade is to give the children something legitimate to do on Halloween instead of keeping the town in an uproar on Halloween with pranks and noise." (Tonia Kissler Cain.)

Wes Tittle and his Tri-County Boys were popular performers in the Redmond area during the 1950s. They were the featured performers at Redmond's (Oregon) Centennial Day celebration dance on April 25, 1959. (Lester Taylor Jr.)

Visit us at
arcadiapublishing.com

www.ingramcontent.com/pod-product-compliance
Lightning Source LLC
Chambersburg PA
CBHW050544110426
42813CB00008B/2251